THE ABINGDON WOMEN'S PREACHING ANNUAL

Series 1

Year A

THE ABINGDON WOMEN'S PREACHING ANNUAL

Series 1

Year A

COMPILED AND EDITED BY

Jana L. Childers and Lucy A. Rose

Abingdon Press
Nashville

THE ABINGDON WOMEN'S PREACHING ANNUAL

Copyright © 1998 by Abingdon Press

This book is printed on recycled, acid-free, elemental-chlorine–free paper.

ISBN 0-687-05709-4
ISSN 1086-8240

Scripture quotations, unless otherwise indicated, are from the New Revised Standard Version Bible, copyright © 1989, by the Division of Christian Education of the National Council of the Churches of Christ in the United States of America.

Scripture quotations noted RSV are from the Revised Standard Version of the Bible, copyright 1946, 1952, 1971 by the Division of Christian Education of the National Council of Churches of Christ in the USA. Used by permission.

Scripture quotations noted KJV are from the King James Version of the Bible.

Scripture quotations noted NASB are from the New American Standard Bible, © The Lockman Foundation 1960, 1962, 1968, 1971, 1972, 1973, 1975, 1977. Used by permission.

Scripture quotations noted NIV are taken from the *Holy Bible: New International Version.* Copyright © 1973, 1978, 1984 by the International Bible Society. Used by permission of Zondervan Bible Publishers.

Scripture quotations noted AT are the author's translation.

The excerpt on p. 59 is from *Guerrillas of Grace* by Ted Loder © 1984. Reprinted by permission of Innisfree Press, Philadelphia, Pa.

The Words of Assurance on p. 64 are adapted from *Book of Worship: United Church of Christ* (New York: UCC Office for Church Life and Leadership, 1986), p. 38.

The excerpt from "The Lone, Wild Bird" on p. 73 is copyright 1927 by *The Homiletic Review.* Used by permission.

The Prayer of Confession on p. 127 is taken from John E. Skoglund and Nancy E. Hall, *A Manual of Worship, New Edition* (Valley Forge, Pa.: Judson Press, 1993), p. 54. Reprinted with permission.

The Assurance of Pardon on p. 156 is from R. Kenneth Ostermiler, in *Book of Worship: United Church of Christ* (New York: UCC Office for Church Life and Leadership, 1986), p. 534.

The excerpt from "Angela" on p. 170 is by Mev Puleo. Copyright 1985 Christian Century Foundation. Reprinted by permission from the April 24, 1985 issue of the Christian Century.

98 99 00 01 02 03 04 05 06 07—10 9 8 7 6 5 4 3 2 1

MANUFACTURED IN THE UNITED STATES OF AMERICA

To

Lucy McIwaine Cook

And

to all the daughters of the promise

who continue to live by the Word

Contents

Introduction

"The Word of the LORD was rare in those days; there was no frequent vision" (I Sam. 3:1 RSV). The writer of I Samuel might just as easily have been talking about the end of the second millennium after Christ as about the opening of the last millennium before his birth.

Over the last few years there has been much speculation about the significance of this particular line in the sands of time. One of the grander theories claims that the two millennia that followed Abraham belonged to God, the two millennia that followed Christ, belonged to him, and that the next two millennia belong to the Holy Spirit. A darker theory projects the Second Coming of Christ at the year that marks two thousand years after his first coming, and which rounds out the second half of salvation history. Perhaps the one generalization that can be made about the effect that crossing the millennial line is having on our culture is that it is making some of us nervous. A tidy schemata, some of us feel, would help.

Regardless of how (and if) you draw the lines, you have to admit the twentieth century is twitching and shuddering its way along to its conclusion. All kinds of people are nervous. The movies are full of apocalyptic imagery—meteors and volcanoes, tornadoes and earthquakes, wars, rumors of war and star wars. All kinds of people are jittery watching the twentieth century draw to a close. And God is not exactly at her loquacious best. Is it true to say that God's word is rare in our day—that there is no frequent vision?

It certainly seems to be true in spots. The institutional Church is fading. Attendance, giving, and enthusiasm are on the wane. The middle-class and upper-middle-class denominations that built A-frame sanctuaries, Danish Modern classrooms, and green-tiled fellowship halls during the midcentury period struggle to keep them half full. Mainline preaching casts about for something else to do now that *narrative preaching* is no longer new. Fewer young men make it as far as the seminary recruitment officer's door. The picture is discouraging. We in the church have long since tired of talking about it. Is there any relief to be had?

There certainly seems to be relief in spots. African-American preaching marches on, like the mighty stream that it is; twelve-step programs point people to God every day; and min-jung and Latin American liberation preachers are reaching many with the vision of Divine justice. Those who have heard a Word from the Lord can pronounce it, it seems. Even in an era such as ours, there are those who manage to press their ear to the right piece of ground, hold their mouths just so, or find an Eli to interpret their experience for them. Interesting, isn't it, how many of them are marked by one kind of marginalization or another? There is something poetic about the fact that as we cross the millennial line, the Word of the Lord is coming to those in the margins.

Even in an age such as ours, there are those who still can hear a Word from the Lord. We need to seek them out. We need to hang on to them when we find them. A little ballyhoo wouldn't hurt. They represent our hope. This book marks the end of Series 1 of the *Abingdon Women's Preaching Annual*. Lucy Rose and I have sought out good listeners and have tried to create a little ballyhoo around their words. We think the Word of God deserves that kind of attention. We dedicate this prayer to the forty-five women listeners whose sermons comprise this series.

Litany of God's Word

LEADER: And the word of the Lord was rare in those days.

PEOPLE: **There was no frequent vision.**

LEADER: Then the king questioned the prophet secretly, "Is there any word from the Lord today?"

PEOPLE: **The prophet said, "There is."**

LEADER: And the word of the Lord came.

PEOPLE: **The word of the Lord came to Samuel.**

LEADER: The word of the Lord came to Ruth.

PEOPLE: **The word of the Lord came to Isaiah.**

LEADER: The word of the Lord came to Rahab.

{ Introduction }

PEOPLE: The word of the Lord came to Daniel.

LEADER: The word of the Lord came to Miriam.

PEOPLE: The word of the Lord came to Ezekiel.

LEADER: The word of the Lord came.

PEOPLE: And Mary said, "Be it unto me according to thy word" (KJV).

LEADER: According to the word of God was the world made

PEOPLE: And the sea parted and the giant slain

LEADER: And the temple built and the walls felled

PEOPLE: And the enemy routed and the city renewed.

LEADER: According to God's word do the lame walk

PEOPLE: And the blind receive their sight

LEADER: And sinners come to believe.

PEOPLE: And the Word became flesh and dwelt among us

LEADER: Full of grace and truth.

PEOPLE: And we have beheld God's glory.

LEADER: Then let us be doers of the word and not hearers only.

PEOPLE: Be it unto us according to God's word.

Jana Childers
Lent 1997
San Anselmo, California

First Sunday of Advent

Anne Miner-Pearson

Isaiah 2:1-5: A picture of the glorified Jerusalem is painted in these verses. It is a city where the Lord shall arbitrate international disputes and the people "shall beat their swords into plowshares."

Psalm 122: A prayer for Jerusalem: "I was glad when they said to me, 'Let us go to the house of the LORD!' "

Romans 13:8-14: The commandments are summed up in the phrase "Love your neighbor as yourself." Since the end is coming soon, Paul exhorts the Romans to live honorably.

Matthew 24:37-44: "For as the days of Noah were, so will be the coming of the Son of Man." The Lord will come suddenly and unexpectedly, Matthew says. It is important to be prepared.

REFLECTIONS

As with all the church's liturgical seasons, Advent works against the American culture. The flow of American life during the four weeks prior to Christmas includes little space for the reflection, repentance, and preparation proclaimed in the lectionary readings. Instead, Christians attempt to live by a spiritual calendar. Often the connection between the rhythms of the church year and the rest of life is difficult to find. At a deeper level, the connection between our faith and the situations of life can be elusive as well. Making that leap between the biblical story and present-day life can be even more difficult than moving between Advent and the mall.

It is this awareness that has shaped the beginning of this sermon. Much of my life is characterized by a kind of disconnection. Fragments and bits of life seem strewn in the wake of numerous activities. Where can we find the link to bind the parts together? What could possibly have the power to connect the separate and sometimes dissociated pieces? Such questions seem appropriate during Advent. It is a season of questions and sharp contrasts. Images of darkness and light, warnings and good news, barrenness and birth stand side by side, making their differences even more pronounced. The task of the preacher is to use those seemingly unrelated contrasts to point the hearers to find God in the "in-between." God has the power to hold it all together.

On this first Sunday of Advent, the Matthew passage speaks of darkness and judgment. The portion from Isaiah speaks of light and hope. The apostle Paul writes to "lay aside the works of darkness and put on the armor of light" (Rom. 13:12*b*). That same Pauline idea is captured in the Episcopal opening prayer for the day: "give us grace to cast away the works of darkness, and put on the armor of light" (*Book of Common Prayer*, 211). The contrasts and strong prophetic tone in all three passages give shape to the sermon. Its voice should echo the prophetic voice. The images need to flow back and forth. And somehow, in the mix, the Good News of God through Jesus Christ should connect the day's message and the lives of the hearers.

In this Advent, the ethnic conflicts throughout the world, such as in Bosnia, fill the news. If the sermon is truly to connect the passages with the present day, it is impossible not to mention these situations. True, the prayers of the people could be used as the vehicle. It is risky business to address controversial political topics from the pulpit, especially when they are current news. The preacher always takes the chance that the hearers will interpret an intended bias or even an unintended one and thus not hear the rest. For those reasons, some preachers shy away from using controversial illustrations.

But, in order to connect the Bible and daily life as well as to point toward the Incarnation we are preparing to celebrate, we must realize the song has ended. Into that bright atmosphere cuts the dark words of Jesus from Matthew. The contrast is jarring to the ear. Yet, in the middle is Jesus. His voice speaks the message: Keep awake.

A SERMON BRIEF

"I want to walk as a child of the light" has all the sweet sounds of Christmas. We sing a wish to be childlike in faith. As the stars are set in the heavens, so Jesus is to be near our star. With the dreamlike hope of a child, we imagine no darkness, a world where light and darkness are "both alike."

There is a small part in all of us that wants to reclaim and hold on to this view of life. How often we wish for life to be simpler. The tugs and pulls of demanding schedules would be smoothed like a wrinkled shirt on the ironing board. How to manage a difficult situation or person would become clear and bright like screwing a new lightbulb into a socket. "I want to walk as a child of the light." Yes, we sing with high soprano voices and with desire in our hearts.

Then the floor drops out from underneath us. The words of Matthew's Gospel sound in our ears. Jesus speaks of dark days. "For as the days of Noah were, so will be the coming of the Son of Man." He reminds us of an unexpected, unplanned-for flood. People are going about their daily lives "eating and drinking, marrying and giving in marriage" (Matt. 24:38). A flood comes, sweeping them all away. Only a few are saved from disaster. Times are no different now, Jesus tells his disciples. The unexpected unplanned-for still happens. Two men are in the field "one will be taken and one will be left. Two women will be grinding meal together; one will be taken and one will be left" (Matt. 24:40).

How unpredictable life is. One day not a cloud in the sky. The next day billowing banks of thunderheads roll your way. For days, months, even years, it rains. The water rises up. You are drowning in a flood.

How mysterious life is. Two seemingly identical situations, decisions, where the people stand side by side. One is blessed. The other fails. "One is taken and the other is left." No matter how hard you try to figure it all out, analyze every factor, consider all contingencies, the unexpected happens.

We sing of light. We know of darkness. We know that only for God there is no darkness at all. Only for God are the day and the night both alike. We live somewhere between the D-flat major chord and a set of discordant notes. We live with rumors of floods, fears of floods, and real floods. We watch as one is taken and the other is left and we have at one time or another been both. Or we are one of the women grinding away at the "meal" of our lives with no guarantee of how our efforts will come out.

Yet, as people of faith, we believe that our life—as dangerous, ambiguous and uncertain as it is—is walked in Christ's light. We are not grinding out our lives each day as meal on a stone. We do not stand in the field defenseless. We pray for God's grace "to lay aside the works of darkness" (Rom. 13:12). We hear Paul tell us to put on the "armor of light" that was given to us in baptism. Our faith is to surround us in the dark.

But there's a trick here, Jesus says. The trick is to keep awake to our faith. The trick is to keep our faith connected with our lives. The trick is to wear the armor of Christ's light into our dangerous, ambiguous and uncertain lives. Either our faith surrounds and holds our lives, or it isn't our faith. Either what we believe becomes part of the discussions and decisions we make, or it will be as if our faith were stolen away in the night. That's the metaphor Jesus uses. There's a thief waiting to catch us asleep so that what is in our "house," our soul, can be taken from us. Keep awake, Jesus says.

The chances to "keep awake," to mix our faith into the frothy brew of our lives, are endless. Chances happen at our job to live out our faith. The "faith test" is put before our teenagers every day. If the current trend continues, one out of five youths today will have AIDS by the age of twenty-nine. Adjust that armor, kids, there are some dark and dangerous choices out there. Dealing with the limitations of an aging body and mind opens the opportunity to grow spiritually. When children or adults try to destroy themselves with food or alcohol because of their own hurts and hopes, we have a chance to move and speak as the "light of Christ."

And, of course, there's Bosnia. Hardly new. We've been praying for that part of the world every Sunday for years. Could there be a more powerful example of a place of darkness? Thousands of people living in fields, in makeshift wagons and tents. Some have only slippers and the thin clothes of summer. Children have been shot in the streets; women raped; and men were marched outside of towns and killed, buried in mass graves. Bosnia seems an endless darkness.

How many conversations did you have about Bosnia this week? How many news programs and newspaper articles offered commentary or additional information to consider? The arguments abound. Sending twenty thousand troops is too few. Twenty thousand is twenty thousand too many because we shouldn't go in there at all. Remember Vietnam—don't go. Remember Nazi Germany—go in. NATO is the only hope. NATO's presence has the potential of stopping the vicious cycle of revenge. Bosnians and Serbs have lived peacefully together and intermarried in the past. They can again. At the height of the debate, the front page of the *Saint Paul Pioneer Press* captured the sense of our nation, I think. The headline read "Worth Fighting For?" and there were three articles below. One in support; another, in protest; the third, the words from the heart of a Croatian poet.

I know congregations are as divided as those columns on the front page of the paper. While none of us would disagree that Bosnia is a place of darkness, the question is what and who will bring light. I have no clearer answer than anyone else, but I believe there must be more to our discussions than the number of troops, the similarity of the past, the historical grip of intolerance.

As people who believe in the light of Christ, Bosnia presents us with a chance to "keep awake" spiritually.

We're being good citizens to argue strategy and feasibility. We need as Christians to struggle with issues of faith. How do we, as Christians, decide if something is "worth fighting for"? Only if no one in our country gets killed? Only if the time line and end result are guaranteed? Only if the people involved appreciate our actions?

What do we, as Christians, do with our fear? Fear can be the midwife of wise choices or the suffocation of new life. How do we "love our neighbor as ourselves" when our neighbor is both a man born in Saginaw and a man born in Sarajevo?

And what about hope? What do we do with hope? We Christians live under the shadow of the Cross, which tells us that even the most powerful darkness of all, death, is not beyond God's redeeming action. We believe God is present in creation, always working to bring peace, reconciliation, and love. Is resurrection only a theological idea that makes for interesting debate, but doesn't apply in Vietnam, Bosnia, or in our lives? Have we fallen asleep and let the thief steal our faith away?

Isaiah speaks of Jerusalem being a light to all nations. He calls his people to draw others to a life of swords changed into plowshares and of spears beaten into pruning hooks. War will not be learned any more. How do we get to a place of not learning war? By using military might to stop a war long enough to establish the structures for peace? Or does engaging in war only reinforce the idea that only war will solve differences?

"Almighty God, give us the grace to cast away the works of darkness, and put upon us the armor of light, now." It is a dark time. Not forgetting the brightness of love and joy we all know, there is more than winter adding darkness to our lives as individuals and as a world. Life has danger. We are never sure of the results of our efforts. We can never know if what we hope will bring love and peace will actually bring that result. We can never be certain that our choices will draw us closer to a fuller life lived in God.

Jesus reminds us that end results are not ours to know—whether in Bosnia or in our own lives. We know no more about the coming of floods than did those neighbors of Noah. The future is no more certain for us than for those two men in the field or the women grinding the meal. But we do know that when we walk in fear and despair, we have fallen asleep. When we consider only national interests and military feasibility, our spiritual house has been broken into. Our armor of light has slipped a little or we've left it in the closet that day. So we need to be wearing our faith in everyday discussions and decisions. We are to live by faith. We are "to walk as a child of the light."

SUGGESTIONS FOR WORSHIP

Call to Worship (Psalm 122 adapted)

LEADER: I was glad when they said to me,

PEOPLE: **"Let us go to the house of the Lord!"**

LEADER: Our feet are standing within your gates, O God.

PEOPLE: **And we pray for the peace of your kingdom.**

LEADER: We gather at your throne, O Lord.

PEOPLE: **And we pray for the well-being of your kingdom.**

LEADER: May they prosper who love you.

PEOPLE: **For the sake of the house of our Lord God, we pray.**

Prayer of Confession

As the days shorten and the nights deepen, our hearts turn to you, O Lord. We sing of light. We know of darkness. We try to follow your path and lose our way. Forgive us for our lip service, our hypocrisies, our wandering after selfish interests. Cast away the works of darkness from us and clothe us in the armor of your light. Lead us through our days and surround us in our nights by the light of your love. Through Jesus Christ our Lord, we pray. Amen.

Assurance of Pardon (I John 1:7 adapted)

LEADER: If we walk in the light, as God is in the light, the blood of Jesus, God's son, cleanses us from all sin. Friends, believe the Good News. In Jesus Christ, we are forgiven.

PEOPLE: Alleluia! Amen!

Charge and Benediction (Rom. 13:11-14 adapted)

Now, you all know what time it is,
Now it is time for us to be awake and stay awake.

For salvation is nearer to us now
Than when we first believed.
Let us then lay aside the works of darkness
And put on the armor of light.
Let us live honorably as children of the day.
Let us love one another, and so fulfill the law of Christ.

Second Sunday of Advent

Barbara Lundblad

Isaiah 11:1-10: "A shoot shall come out from the stump of Jesse." This poetic picture of the Davidic dynasty offers a vision of the realm of God where the wolf shall "lie down with the lamb" (KJV).

Psalm 72:1-7, 18-19: A prayer that the king may rule in justice: "In his days may righteousness flourish and peace abound until the moon is no more."

Romans 15:4-13: Paul makes a plea for the Christians in Rome—Jews and Gentiles—to live together in harmony.

Matthew 3:1-12: The passage recounts the preaching of John the Baptist: "Repent . . . even now the ax is lying at the root of the trees."

REFLECTIONS

In this sermon I do something I seldom do—preach on one verse of one lectionary text. Isaiah 11 overflows with wondrous images: the tiny shoot growing from a stump, the anointing of the spirit of the Lord (words that we pray at baptism and reception of members in Lutheran congregations), the uncompromising promise to bring justice for the poor, and the glorious vision of the peaceable kingdom. What do we do with such a feast in one lesson? Then, there is Matthew 3, John the Baptist's strong call to repentance that recalls words from Isaiah 40 and at least a hint of the stump of Isaiah 11 with his warning about the ax laid even now at the root of the trees.

As I listened not only to these scripture texts but also to the text of this congregation, I made the decision to focus on the small sign growing from the root of Jesse. The days from Thanksgiving to Christmas (that is, Advent) are the hardest time of the year for many. In this particular year, I heard more than the usual amount of pain. Thus, I longed for people to be surprised by small signs in their wilderness. I moved outside Isaiah 11:1 to make connections with the earlier word of judgment in chapter 3, as well as the later Servant Song (Isaiah 53) in which the servant is a young plant growing out of dry ground. I moved from the biblical shoot to a nature image that people here know, then to a corollary image beyond nature (the man in mourning), and finally to a corporate image of African-American people breaking through oppression and stereotypes to sing in the sunlight for all to hear. Isaiah's other images will have to wait for three years to be preached, although the congregation did hear them as they were read and will carry them along as they move through the Advent season.

A Sermon Brief

"A shoot shall come out from the stump of Jesse, and a branch shall grow."

"Wait!" I cry. "It cannot be." For I have seen the stump, clean cut in the farmyard where I grew up. "Such a wonderful old tree," we said, "too bad it had to go." For years we said the same thing, but now we just sit where the tree was. The stump is solid, smoothed by the saw that severed it from the last trace of green. We try to count the rings, but we do not expect the stump to grow. Not even one tiny shoot. The stump is dead. The prophet had warned that it would be so; the word was clear:

The LORD enters into judgment
  with the elders and princes of his people:
It is you who have devoured the vineyard;
  the spoil of the poor is in your houses.
What do you mean by crushing my people,
  by grinding the face of the poor? says the Lord GOD of hosts. (Isa. 3:14-15)

The word had come from God: This tree must be cut down. Severed. Perhaps later many will come and count the rings of the stump, trying to remember if this tree, or this people ever really existed. The tree, the people. Both will be clean cut.

And yet, another word comes, from the very same prophet. "A shoot shall come out from the stump of Jesse." Can we even imagine such a thing? Do we dare to believe the prophet's word as we sit on the stump waiting?

Sometimes, I have seen glimpses of such a promise, of something growing where nothing should. Perhaps you have seen it, too. It has been ten years since the new police station was built in my neighborhood in New York City. I often stopped to watch when the digging began. "They'll never finish this," I said to no one but myself. For Manhattan is a mighty rock—a rock holding up the Empire State Building and rows of housing projects. A rock carved into tunnels for subways and pipes, and holding up over a million people coming and going. Such a rock does not give in easily. I watched them try by using hulking machines with jackhammers bigger than buses. Up, up they lifted the hammers, then down with a deafening crash, making barely a dent. Again and again, day after day, until finally cracks appeared on the surface. Those same rocks now form the park where I go jogging (when its not raining or snowing or too hot!). They stand like sentinels over the Hudson River—rocks that make a mockery of jackhammers.

And yet I have seen something else along the path. A tiny seedling pushing out into the sunlight. A tender shoot no bigger than my finger breaks through the rock without the aid of a jackhammer. There are, I know, scientific explanations why such a thing is possible, yet each time I see it, that stubborn shoot appears to me a miracle.

Perhaps you have seen it too. A blade of grass so stubborn it breaks through the concrete sidewalk, growing precisely where it shouldn't. Or maybe you have seen something else, not rock or tree, but a sight more fragile still.

There is a man on my street, a man I've known for years. We often met in the early morning at the newsstand. Last year, his wife died. Forty-two years together were reduced to loneliness. He no longer came to the newsstand. I watched him walking, his head bowed, his shoulders drooping lower each day. His whole body seemed in mourning, cut off from me and others on the street. I grew accustomed to saying, "Good morning," without any response. Until a week ago. Before I could say a word he turned to me and said, "Good morning, Reverend. Going for your paper?" He walked beside me, his face alive, eager to talk. He seemed transformed. I could not know what brought the change that seemed so sudden. No doubt, for him, it wasn't sudden at all, but painfully slow. Like a seedling pushing through rock toward the sunlight. Perhaps he could have given me reasons—time passing, open wounds beginning to heal. There surely must have been an explanation, yet he appeared to me a miracle.

We often decide far too soon where things can't grow. "Surely not there!" we say. The rock's too hard, the light too dim, the stump too dead. Across the river from Manhattan's rock, Jersey City clings to the edge of the Hudson. My friend Ruth grew up there in the '30s. She told me it wasn't so bad growing up as a Black person in Jersey City in those years. If you were light-skinned enough and straightened your hair, you could get a good job—especially at the phone company, which is exactly what her mother did.

Every Saturday afternoon as soon as the weather was warm, Ruth and her mother Mabel would get all dressed up. They'd put on their best clothes, fit for the finest party in town. But they didn't even go out the door. They put two chairs on the fire escape and left the windows wide open, with the radio inside tuned to the Saturday afternoon broadcast from the Metropolitan Opera. Mabel knew most of the arias by heart—she sang along with her favorites. Ruth had most of them memorized by the time she was in junior high.

One day, Mabel overheard some White folks at work say that Black people could never understand opera. Mabel would tell that story and laugh until tears rolled down her face, then often she would break into an aria. And she surely was pleased when Marian Anderson was invited to sing on the steps of the Lincoln Memorial.

People didn't expect much to grow in that part of Jersey City. But hope can be stubborn; you can try to keep people down, you can put all kinds of obstacles in their way, yet they push through the sidewalk. They break through the rock where the jackhammers failed, and they sing in the sunlight for all in the streets to hear.

"A shoot shall come out from the stump of Jesse, and a branch shall grow out of his roots." Who could believe such a word in the midst of judgment and ruin? Who could imagine anything growing as they sat on the stump of utter despair, counting the rings of the past?

I've sat there myself, and perhaps you have, too. You may be there now, at that place where hope is cut off, where loss and despair have deadened your heart. God's Advent word comes to sit with you. This word will not ask you to get up and dance. The prophet's vision is surprising, but small. The nation would never rise again. Things would never be the same. The stump would not become a mighty cedar. The shoot that was growing, the branch coming from Jesse's root would be different from what they had known or expected:

> For he grew up before him like a young plant,
>   and like a root out of dry ground;
> he had no form or majesty that we should look at him,
>   nothing in his appearance that we should desire him.
> He was despised and rejected by others. (Isa. 53:2-3*a*)

A plant out of dry ground, a sprig of green where all was cut off. Can we believe the prophet's words? Some dared to hold that vision in their hearts. They no longer saw only the stump, but the tender shoot growing. They believed this shoot would grow, in spite of all evidence to the contrary. It would grow out of the very pain of the past. That pain would not be denied, nor would it ever go away. But despair would not be the final word. A shoot will grow from the stump of Jesse. Fragile, it was, yet tenacious and stubborn. It would grow out of dry ground, it would push back the stone from the rock-hard tomb.

It will grow in the heart of a man cut off by sorrow, until one morning he can look up again and tip his hat. It will grow in the hearts of people told over and over that they are nothing. And though the pain and anger do not go away, they believe God's promise is stronger than the so-called owners of this world. The plant will grow; it will break through places where jackhammers failed. It will sing on the fire escape and soar from the steps of the Lincoln Memorial.

It will grow in you, too, and in me. Precisely in that place where hope is cut off. Oh, I would like a bigger sign, and probably you would, too. But what if we dare to trust that the tender shoot is growing? What if we believe this too-small sign is God's beginning? Perhaps then we would tend the seedling in our hearts, the place where faith longs to break through the hardness of our disbelief.

Do not wait for the tree to be full grown. God comes to you and me in this Advent time and invites us to move beyond counting the rings of the past. We may still want to sit on the stump for a while, and God will sit with us. But God will keep nudging us saying: "Look! Look there on the stump. . . . Do you see the sprig of green?"

SUGGESTIONS FOR WORSHIP

Call to Worship

LEADER: A shoot shall come out from the stump of Jesse,

PEOPLE: And a branch shall grow out of his roots.

LEADER: Hope shall come forth out of despair,

PEOPLE: And boldness shall shake us from apathy.

LEADER: Rejoicing shall break forth after nights of weeping,

PEOPLE: And the song of God shall be heard again in our land.

LEADER: Open our eyes to the small shoot growing;

PEOPLE: Open our ears to the prophet's word;

LEADER: Open our hearts to visions we cannot imagine:

PEOPLE: Come, Lord Jesus. Come.

Prayer of Confession

The prophets and John the Baptist call us to turn away from sin, to amend our lives and hold fast to the promises of God. As we prepare for Christ's coming, let us confess our sin against God and one another.

A time of silence for reflection and self-examination.

(*Resume prayer in unison.*) Faithful God, we confess to you that we have not trusted your signs of hope in our midst. We have looked for bigger signs and easier answers. We have given up too quickly; we have grown impatient in our waiting. Forgive us for turning away from you and from one another. Forgive us for failing to trust that you are with us. Come to us now and grant us your peace. Amen.

Assurance of Pardon

Sisters and brothers, God is faithful and will not hold our sins against us. God's mercy is larger than our forgetfulness and deeper than our despair. God forgives us all our sins and grants us newness of life. Even now God's grace is springing up within us like a tender plant. Behold: Now is the day of salvation. Amen.

Benediction

May the Spirit of the living God rest upon you:
the spirit of wisdom and understanding,
the spirit of counsel and might,
the spirit of knowledge and the fear of the Lord. Amen.

Third Sunday of Advent

Joanna Dewey

Isaiah 35:1-10: Many blessings are prophesied for Israel: the desert shall blossom, the eyes of the blind shall be opened, a way shall be made in the wilderness.

Luke 1:47-55: Mary's Magnificat recounts God's mighty words.

James 5:7-10: Believers are urged to have patience for the coming of the Lord, as the prophets did.

Matthew 11:2-11, 16-19: John the Baptist sends his disciples to ascertain Jesus' identity. Jesus replies by listing what his ministry has accomplished, then turns to the crowd around him to make sure they know the significance of Jesus' ministry.

REFLECTIONS

Last Sunday, the second Sunday of Advent, we read about the coming of John the Baptist and his preaching of judgment on the Jewish leaders. We heard his thundering denunciation of the Pharisees and the Sadduccees; his prophecy of the coming judgment of God on all humanity. "You spawn of Satan! Who warned you to flee from the impending doom?" (Matt. 3:7 AT). "Even now the ax is aimed at the root of the trees; so every tree not producing choice fruit gets cut down and tossed into the fire" (v. 10 AT). "I baptize you with water to signify a change of heart, but one who is more powerful than I is coming after me; one whose sandals I am not worthy to carry. That one will baptize you with the Holy Spirit and fire" (v. 11 AT). "God's pitchfork is ready, God will make a clean sweep of the threshing floor and will gather the wheat into the granary, but the chaff God will burn in a fire that can't be put out" (v. 12 AT).

Present day Sadducees, that is, those from our very top political-economic echelons; and present day Pharisees, that is, many of us who are middle-class functionaries enjoying the benefits of a first-world society—we all still stand under John's threat of judgment, we too need to heed the warning to flee from God's wrath.

In today's Gospel lesson we hear Matthew's version of Jesus' response to John. John, now in prison, sends word to Jesus to ask who he is. And according to Matthew 11:45, Jesus responds by enumerating the fulfillment of the blessings prophesied by Isaiah in our first reading:

> "Go and report to John what you hear and see, the blind see again and the lame walk, lepers are cleansed and the deaf hear, the dead are raised, and the destitute have good news brought to them. Congratulations to those who do not take offense at me." (AT)

And we, too, in all of our struggles and pain, are being offered the blessings of God's realm, healing, rejoicing, and partying with food in abundance.

John's message focused on judgment and wrath, especially judgment and wrath on those with some power and status in their society. In contrast, Jesus' message and actions focused on *good* news, now, especially for those without power or status in their society, for those caught in pain and suffering.

A Sermon Brief

Both John the Baptist and Jesus proclaim God's invitation to join God's realm. John threatens doom if we do not; Jesus offers blessings, hope, healing, and joy, since God's realm has already begun. Indeed Matthew 3:2 and 4:17 present their opening proclamations in words conveying an identical message: "Change your ways because heaven's rule is closing in."

Both John and Jesus proclaim God's reign, and in today's Gospel, Jesus tells of his extremely high esteem for John: "I swear to you, among those born of women, no one has arisen who is greater than John the Baptist" (Matt. 11:11 AT). Jesus, also born of woman, does not even exempt himself.

But he goes on to say, "Yet the least in heaven's domain is greater than he." Any of us, all of us, here and there and throughout the world, even the least of us, is as important—or as unimportant—as John, if only we enter God's domain.

And there is where the Gospel lesson officially ends. But I have continued with four more verses. If your knowledge of the Bible is only from Sunday readings you have never heard these verses, even though they occur here in Matthew, and also in Luke. For they never occur in a Sunday lectionary reading.

I have included these verses, because they call us to respond from the depths of our beings to the call of God, as it came through John the Baptist, as it came through Jesus, as it continues to come through Christ, through the Holy Spirit:

> What does this generation remind me of? It is like children sitting in market-places who call out to others, "We played the flute for you, but you would not dance; we sang a dirge, but you would not mourn." (AT)

We played the flute for you, but you would not dance.

That is, We said, Come play wedding, party, feast, rejoicing, and you sat there, you would not rejoice.

We sang a dirge but you wouldn't mourn.

That is, We said, come play funeral, fasting, weeping, grieving, sorrowing, and you sat there, you would not mourn.

So Jesus compared the women and men of his day to children playing: they wouldn't respond to John who fasted and mourned—they called him a sugar addict, an alcoholic, a crony of extortionists and pimps. They would neither rejoice nor grieve.

And so often, still, we are like that today, responding neither to the call to joy nor to the call to grieve. As individuals we sit on our emotions, deny our feelings, hide them even from ourselves. We know that grieving for the sins of our past or for the pains of our world will hurt, so we repress our awareness for fear the hurt will destroy us—and we shut out God along with the pain. We often try to avoid change; we risk it only with difficulty and fear. But that change might bring us joy, might bring us God. And we rarely dare to rejoice, for we know at some level to let joy in is also to let in pain, and we cannot be open to joy without also being open to suffering; that is the way we are made. So we dare not rejoice, and again we shut out God.

As a culture we run away from responding; we avoid being aware—so that we do not have to rejoice, so that we do not have to mourn. Perhaps more so at Advent and Christmastime than any other time we silence our response by the characteristically American, time-honored and very efficient method of being very busy: we have project topics to choose, papers to write, papers to correct, presents to buy and get in the mail, Christmas cards to write, packing to be done, planes to catch, and meals to cook. We have no time to feel, to experience the joy of Christmas and the tragedy of the world and what is to come. Indeed, we may even be too busy to notice that we have not grieved and prepared for Christ's coming to this Advent, that we are not rejoicing in Christ's birth this Christmas. We are too busy to respond, even to let ourselves become conscious that we are not responding. It's scary to respond. And we are right to be scared. Still, it is the way to God, to hope and life. But often as not, as the Holy One calls us anew each Advent and Christmas, we still are like the children in the marketplace, choosing neither to grieve nor rejoice.

As the Episcopal Church, we are not very comfortable with either grief or joy. We prefer things done decently and in order, with staid and formal propriety. We want to keep a proper face on things at all times. Even our weddings and funerals tend to be proper affairs. Our church is often like the children in the marketplace who will neither dance nor weep. And as such, we keep God's call to us to respond at a nice safe distance, neither rejoicing nor weeping ourselves, nor calling the world to weep and rejoice with us.

So I call to us all *this Advent,* to dare to let in a little more rejoicing, to try dancing a step or two, alone and together. And I call us this Advent to dare to mourn a little more—to try shedding a tear or two, supporting one another. The Holy One calls us still today, as John and Jesus called to the people of Galilee and Judea long ago. Let us not be like the children in the marketplace; let us grieve and weep, let us sing and dance. Let us dare to respond to God. Amen.

Suggestions for Worship

Call to Worship (Ps. 146:5-10 adapted)

LEADER: Happy are those who have the eternal God for their help.

PEOPLE: **Whose help is in the name of the Lord.**

LEADER: Truly our hope is in God.

PEOPLE: **Who made heaven and earth and all therein.**

LEADER: Who stands with the oppressed and feeds the hungry.

PEOPLE: **Who looses prisoners and opens the eyes of the blind.**

LEADER: Our God raises those who are bound down.

PEOPLE: And loves the righteous, the stranger, the orphan, and the widow.

LEADER: But the way of the wicked God turns upside down.

PEOPLE: Our God reigns forever. Praise the Lord.

Prayer of Confession

Gracious God, to whom all hearts are open and from whom no secrets are hidden, we confess that we are uneasy being known and seen by you. We prefer the safer path, the middle way, the noncommittal response. We like to be in charge of what we disclose about ourselves. Preserving our dignity has been important to us. But you, O God, know our longing and our losses—our joys and our delights. Blow on the coals of our hearts, we pray, that we might be delivered to a deeper love and a freer life. Through Jesus Christ our Lord. Amen.

Assurance of Pardon

LEADER: Whoever is in Christ is a new creation altogether.
The past is finished and gone.
Everything has become fresh and new.
Friends, believe the Good News.

PEOPLE: In Jesus Christ we are forgiven.
Alleluia! Amen.

Benediction

Great is the Lord
Who comes to save us:
Who heals and clears a path for us,
Who raises rosebushes in the midst of our deserts,
Who protects us in going forth
And who brings us home.
Who can resist such a God?

Christmas Day

Cynthia Hale

Isaiah 9:2-7: God's promise of light for those in darkness and exuberant joy. God's promise also of a child who will be "Wonderful Counselor, Mighty God, Everlasting Father, Prince of Peace."

Psalm 96: A call to all the peoples to sing a new song to God, to worship and praise God. And a call to all the heavens, the earth, the sea, the fields, and the trees to sing for joy for God is coming.

Titus 2:11-14: Paul's charge to live godly lives as we wait for the revealing of the glory of God and our Savior Jesus Christ.

Luke 2:1-14 (15-20): Luke's story of the birth of Jesus.

REFLECTIONS

In Luke 2:1-20, the angels and the shepherds worshiped and praised God. So too had Elizabeth and Mary earlier in Luke's story. At the angel's word that Mary's kinswoman Elizabeth, in her old age, was also pregnant, Mary traveled from Nazareth to Judea, entered the house, and greeted Elizabeth. At this point in the story Mary was not singing praises. Had she come for protection, for comfort? The angel Gabriel told Mary she was about to have a baby. That may be good news to a married woman who has been praying for, preparing for, and trying to have a baby with her husband. But Mary wasn't married; she was engaged. The marriage had not been consummated. Mary wasn't even sexually active; she was a virgin. But who would believe that, especially when they saw that she was pregnant?

According to Luke's story, when Elizabeth heard Mary's greeting, the baby that was in her womb leaped and Elizabeth began to bless Mary and her baby, confirming that she was carrying the son of God as the angel had said. What a confirmation! So mighty was the presence of God-with-us in Mary that both Elizabeth and the baby in her womb reacted in jubilation. They couldn't help themselves. It's like that when you are in the presence of God and you know it.

And Mary, upon receiving this confirmation and blessing, exploded into a psalm of praise to God. I use the word *exploded* because this was no quiet, timid expression of joy. In 1:46, the King James Version states that Mary sang, "My soul doth magnify the Lord." The New International Version says, "My soul glorifies the Lord." The New American Standard says, "My soul exalts the Lord." Magnifying, glorifying, exalting the Lord—this is the language of worship and praise. "My spirit," continues Mary, according to the New International Version, "rejoices in God my Savior." The Greek word here for *rejoice* is *agellian*. It means spiritual exaltation or sacred rapture. It describes the experience of being carried away in divine ecstasy. It is the joy of worship in which God is experienced and praised.

Mary's praise is expressed with her lips, but it comes from down deep within. This is no mere lip service. Mary's words are an expression of what is going on inside of her as she experiences God's revelation on the inside.

True worship and praise first come from within. God draws near to us. God becomes up close and personal. God becomes Immanuel—with us and in us. At Christmas we praise and worship our God who has come to us in a personal and real way in Jesus.

A SERMON BRIEF

Another Christmas! How tempting to celebrate in the same old way. How tempting for me to preach a nice little sermon on the Christmas story and let everyone go home to continue business as usual. But I can't. There's more to the season than Christmas trees and gifts, turkeys and hams, eggnog and entertaining family and friends for a day or two. There's more to this whole Christmas scene than we seem to realize. We all—I say "we all," but perhaps I shouldn't put everyone together here. Anyway, most of us seem to miss the whole point of Christmas and what our attitude should be throughout and because of the season. We understand, at least superficially, that Jesus is the reason for the season. But it's obvious that we don't understand the significance of Jesus' coming to earth as did those who were present at the first Christmas. If we did, then we would act as they did.

When I read the Christmas story recorded in Luke, and also in Matthew, what is most clear to me is that the news that a baby was about to be born or had been born in Bethlehem brought a reaction of great joy, worship, and praise from all who heard it, regardless of their life situations. The birth narratives of Jesus are permeated with praise and filled with worship from a cast of characters. There are God's heavenly host, as well as the heathen kings who came to pay him homage. There are those who were illiterate, as well as those who could analyze the patterns and positions of the stars. The promise and proclamation of a baby's birth brought them joy and evoked worship, for this was no ordinary baby but Immanuel, God-with-us.

Scholar Evelyn Underhill, in her book *Worship,* defines worship as "the total adoring response of [humans] to . . . God." The phrase "adoring response" says that worship is personal and passionate, not formal and cold. Worship engages us with the living God and is our response to God's presence in our midst. To qualify this "adoring response" with the adjective *total* is to say that worship is the Christian's balanced response of all that he or she is—mind, emotions, will, and body—to all that God is, says, and does.

Now, too often we want to relegate worship and praise to a set time, place, and manner. We expect to go to church to worship. Then, when we get there to "worship," we need external stimuli to get us going. Does this sound familiar? If the choir doesn't sing right, then you haven't worshiped. If the right preacher isn't preaching or if the preacher didn't preach right, then you haven't worshiped.

But it wasn't in a church that the angels or the shepherds worshiped and praised God. Instead worship needs to happen at all times and anywhere. Everything we do ought to bring glory to God. It's true that the psalmist says, "Enter his gates with thanksgiving, and his courts with praise" (100:4*a*). But the psalmist suggests that we ought to be worshiping and thanking God *before* we get to church! We need to arrive worshiping.

We can praise God anywhere. In Luke's Christmas narrative, the angels who appeared to the shepherds worshiped and praised God in midair. The great company of the heavenly host, hovering in the air, burst forth

> "Glory to God in the highest heaven,
>   and on earth peace among those whom he favors!" (Luke 2:14)

Then the angels left, and the shepherds hurried off to Bethlehem. They found things just as the angel had said; the promised baby was there in the manger. And when they had seen him, what was their response? They "returned, glorifying and praising God for all they had heard and seen, as it had been told them" (Luke 2:20). Another case of "I just couldn't keep it to myself what the Lord has done for me."

The only way we can possibly keep quiet about this Christmas event is if we do not know God. If God has not revealed himself to you, then you would have nothing to rejoice about. But when God reveals himself to you, when God becomes real to you, when God becomes with you—Immanuel—in your heart, when God saves your soul, there is no other response than worship, rejoicing, glorifying, and praising God.

The baby born in the manger grew up to become our Savior. The angels announced to the shepherds, "To you is born this day in the city of David a Savior, who is the Messiah, the Lord" (Luke 2:11). Our Savior, Jesus, came to redeem us, to reconcile us to God, to make a personal, praise-filled relationship with God possible.

And what does God want in return? God wants your heart. God wants a heart that will praise him, a heart that will rejoice like the psalmist:

> I will praise you, O LORD, with all my heart;
> I will tell of all your wonders.
> I will be glad and rejoice in you;
> I will sing praise to your name, O Most High. (9:1-2 NIV)

When our hearts are surrendered to God in worship and praise, everything else follows. If the attitude of each heart is worship and praise, then we will worship at all times, in all places.

Paul's response to God for the gift of his son is recorded in 2 Corinthians 9:15: "Thanks be to God for his indescribable gift." This should be our response, our attitude, at Christmas and always. If our hearts are not overwhelmed with gratitude and adoration, then we have missed the whole point of Christmas.

Worship is the first order of the day at Christmas! O come, let us adore him, O come, let us adore him, Christ, the Lord.

SUGGESTIONS FOR WORSHIP

Call to Worship

O come, let us adore him,. O come, let us adore him, O come, let us adore him, Christ, the Lord.

Prayer of Confession (in unison)

O God, forgive us when the extras of Christmas overshadow its essence. Forgive us when the trappings of Christmas—the tree, the presents, the guests, the decorations—detract from the simple story of a baby born in a manger. Forgive us when our songs of praise to You are drowned out by the rush and hurriedness of the season. Forgive us when memories of Christmases past crowd out the possibility of your presence as God-with-us now. Forgive us, for in Jesus Christ you came to redeem us and to reconcile us to yourself.

Assurance of Pardon

The manger baby grew up. He healed the brokenhearted, forgave sinners, raised the dead, and gave his life that we might be set free from our sins and live new, praise-filled lives. In Jesus Christ we are forgiven.

Ascription of Praise and Benediction (Luke 2:14)

"Glory to God in the highest heaven,
    and on earth peace among those whom he favors!"

May God's peace rest among you and within you, the peace of Immanuel, God-with-us.

Epiphany

Minerva Carcaño

Isaiah 60:1-6: God's light has come to Zion and all nations will be drawn to it. "They shall bring gold and frankincense, and shall proclaim the praise of the LORD."

Psalm 72:1-7, 10-14: The rule of a righteous king is celebrated. The kings of numerous countries bow before him.

Ephesians 3:1-12: The passage describes Paul's ministry to the Gentiles. "It has now been revealed . . . the Gentiles have become fellow heirs."

Matthew 2:1-12: The wise men from the East come to Jerusalem seeking the king of the Jews. After meeting with Herod, they follow the star and discover Mary and Jesus.

REFLECTIONS

What a wonder it is to be able to celebrate the manifestation of God in human life. Prophesied generations before through the lips of Isaiah (60:1-6), God shines upon all creation in the birth of Jesus. While some expect a demonstration of power of the kind that forcefully conquers and dominates, the Creator chooses the power of birth, the mystery of new life, the helpless tenderness of a babe born in a manger, to announce hope and salvation fulfilled. It is a most unexpected Epiphany of the One in whose hands all things abide.

It is a different world indeed when God reigns. The psalmist (72:1-7, 10-14) understood the difference. God cares for the well-being of the people; their "shalom" is of utmost importance. Thus, rulers committed to the guiding presence and direction of God, rule with the heart of God dispensing justice and righteousness, understanding themselves to be the deliverers of the poor, the weak, and the needy, on behalf of God. In the coming of Jesus, the world is blessed and disquieted as he, the perfect king, reveals not only repair for social orders gone amuck, but calls persons to an order beyond those we yet know, where true wholeness can be experienced.

Not least among the characteristics of this new social order is the unity of all people. The apostle Paul captures the message well in stating that through Jesus Christ, Jews and Gentiles alike "have become fellow heirs, members of the same body, and sharers in the promise in Christ Jesus through the gospel" (Eph. 3:6). It is no mere poetic imagery when the prophet Isaiah many generations before proclaimed that the day would come when the nations would gather round Israel—beckoned there by God's light emanating through Israel. The manifestation of God in human history through the birth of the Christ Child brings healing to all God's children as they are reconciled with God and with one another.

Seekers of healing and wholeness who search for the one "born king of the Jews" and of all people, will be led by none other than God. The Magi (Matt. 2:1-12) were such seekers. The Magi, astrologers given to the religious doctrine of Zoroaster, were an unusual choice to be among those who first discover the coming of God, but their earnestness in finding the God child and their humility in worshiping him, earn them a place in the great story of faith. Through a star, the words of the prophet Micah, and a dream, God leads the Magi to the revelation of the Good News that God's light has shone and the darkness of human life has been dispelled. With good reason the Magi are filled with joy and pay homage to the eternal king through gifts of gold, frankincense, and myrrh.

Not all welcome the light, however. King Herod is afraid along with all the people of Jerusalem. Who is this "king of the Jews," announced by the stars? Whose power does he pretend to assume? He may be able to fool silly Magi, but he will not fool King Herod! Darkness is the preferred state of some whose evil would be revealed in the shining of the true Light. A time of oppressive tyranny such as was the time of King Herod was the good time of God's Epiphany! It is a wonder to behold, all the more so as we remember that the Epiphany that we celebrate is God's great gift of grace to us.

A SERMON BRIEF

The children were excited about the church Epiphany celebration. Christmas was over but there was one more fun program and party. The most unruly boys were to be the three Wise Men, chosen as a way to keep them under control. A chubby, shy twelve-year-old girl would be Mary. A constant baby-sitter for her three younger siblings, she knew how to hold a baby. The tallest boy would be King Herod and the rest of the children would be an odd assortment of palace guards, priests, scribes, shepherds, and angels. Rehearsals were rough, but there was no turning back since the announcement of a family Epiphany activity had gone out at the beginning of Advent.

The children were from Mexico, Central America, and Cuba. Many of them were undocumented aliens. All of them lived in a quadrant of the city called "the war zone" because of its violence. These children and their families lived in utter poverty. For many of them, the only Christmas gift received was the one the church had given them at its children's Christmas party. Epiphany was a new thing for them, but it gave them something to do and a chance to enjoy a refreshment of sweet bread and juice.

It was strange that the children had no awareness of Epiphany since the afternoon's program was based on the biblical story of the visit of the Wise Men, but was being celebrated in the Mexican tradition of the "Fiesta de los Reyes Magos." I found it interesting that the Mexican children with their families had come to a foreign land to celebrate a tradition of their homeland. I wondered what they must hold in common with the Magi, also foreigners celebrating the birth of Jesus in a strange land.

After a pageant-style presentation of the biblical story of the visit of the Wise Men, the children and their families gathered in the fellowship hall to play games and enjoy the traditional Mexican sweet bread known as Wise Men's Bread—a bread shaped in a ring meant to remind those who eat it of the Wise Men's crowns. In each bread is hidden a miniature baby doll representing the baby Jesus. The baby doll is baked right into the bread and the person whose slice of bread has the baby doll is crowned with a decorative crown that announces that he or she has, like the Magi, found the Son of God, the Light of the World.

It was a great afternoon. Once again, God's presence had transformed simple efforts into moments of glorious joy. The children were proud of their pageant and content with their full stomachs. Tomorrow they would again experience the darkness of poverty, of drug abuse, and gang violence, but for the moment they glowed with the light of Christ.

It is to the children that we must again strive to teach the story of God's Epiphany. It is not sufficient to teach them the story of the birth of the Christ Child, of the Incarnation of God who has chosen to be present with us.

Children, along with adults, need to hear the message of Epiphany: that the light of God incarnate shines for all humanity, breaking through all darkness. With the Magi we are invited to follow Christ's light and to allow it to shine through us.

One of the children in the Epiphany celebration heard the message and responded to it. With two brothers in jail awaiting trial in a drug-related murder, this young child of ten began to pray on his own. "Pastor, I want Jesus to live in me," he would say when I visited his home. "Follow Jesus," I would counsel him. Though not a perfect child, he began to grow and mature in his faith and we began to see the radiance of God's grace and Christ's love in his life.

I worry about this child, knowing as I do, the circumstances of his life with its violence and want. In my worry I am drawn again to the Matthean story. If the light of Christ is able to penetrate the darkness of the terror of Herod—who had two of his sons murdered because he suspected them of conspiracy, and also had a wife murdered along with hundreds of public servants for various other suspicions—can it not break through the darkness of modern manifestations of horror and oppression? But it is better than that. The star of Bethlehem points to the One who penetrates all darkness, transforming human life and restoring it to right relationship with God and with all of creation. Through God's abiding grace, children can dream and expect a better world.

A child touched to belief by a play and a baby doll in his bread. It is not so unusual when we consider that Mary the mother of Jesus came to understand the Light within her through the help of Elizabeth, her cousin and friend; that the fishermen of Galilee saw Jesus' light after a miraculous catch; and that for the Magi, men who consulted the heavenly beings, God's revelation would come through a star. Epiphany is a day of eternal hope, for not only is God shattering the pain, the affliction, the alienation, the suffering, and all that keeps us in darkness, God is faithfully reaching out to each one of us where we are, speaking to us through the common and the known, so that none of us are left in darkness or without salvation.

One dark evening I arrived at the "war zone." I was going to pray with the family of the child who wanted Jesus to live in him. One of his imprisoned brothers was about to go to trial. We gathered in the family's small living room, making a circle and holding hands to pray together. As I prayed, the ten-year-old child could be heard saying softly, "Thank you Jesus." When we finished praying the child looked up at me and smiled and the room lit up with his confidence and joy in Christ. In remembering that evening, I have come to a better understanding of the joy of the Magi, who, though they journeyed under the darkness of the evil watch of Herod, were able to rejoice upon finding the Christ Child. The Magi experienced the touch of Christ's redeeming light, discovering that when we abide in this sacred light we will not be overcome. Even a child knows this.

SUGGESTIONS FOR WORSHIP

Call to Worship

LEADER: See, the light of hope is upon us!

PEOPLE: **Rejoice in the coming of God!**

LEADER: We were once a people who lived in darkness, but now we see.

PEOPLE: **Righteousness, justice, and prosperity are pouring down upon God's people.**

LEADER: The poor are defended, the needy are delivered, and the oppressor is crushed.

PEOPLE: **Yes, the darkness of evil is dispelled and the light of Redemption shines.**

LEADER: It shines brightly for Magi, for shepherds, for Mary and Joseph, for Jew and Gentile.

PEOPLE: **It shines leading homeward to the place where God reigns gathering her children.**

LEADER: Come and see the light: the Baby Jesus lying in a manger, Immanuel, God with us.

PEOPLE: **Bring him gifts of gold, frankincense, and myrrh.**

LEADER: Bring him your hearts and be filled with his radiance.

PEOPLE: **Proclaim the praise of the Lord!**

Prayer of Confession (in unison)

God of everlasting light, we confess that often we prefer the darkness to living in your light. We resist the disruption that your presence causes in our living. We seek after those things that would bring us comfort and glory, ignoring the needs of those around us and thus ignoring you. And we have no peace, comfort, or joy. Forgive us Lord, and bathe us in your redeeming light. Make us whole again with spirits of righteousness and justice. Take us by the hand and guide us to your salvation. Hide not, O God, your radiance. Be merciful toward us and shine with all your glory. Amen.

Assurance of Pardon

Look anew and know that God is merciful, caring for us even in the midst of our rebellion. Seek the Light and it will be found, for God's eternal plan is our redemption. Lift up your heads, forgiven of God, and rejoice in your salvation.

Benediction

LEADER: We have known God's light, let us now go and share it.

PEOPLE: **We go committed to being bearers of God's light of mercy and justice.**

LEADER: Go and radiate the love of God, calling God's people home.

PEOPLE: **May the Spirit of light and love go with us till we reach the day of God's eternal reign.**

Baptism of the Lord (Ordinary Time 1)

Minerva Carcaño

Isaiah 42:1-9: These nine verses comprise one of four "servant songs." The servant is given by God as a "light to the nations."

Psalm 29: This hymn celebrates God's voice breaking through a thunderstorm.

Acts 10:34-43: Peter preaches the Good News of God's impartiality.

Matthew 3:13-17: Jesus persuades a reluctant John the Baptist to baptize him. A dove alights on Jesus and a voice from heaven pronounces him the Son of God.

REFLECTIONS

The central focus of this first Sunday after the Epiphany is the baptism of Jesus. The first of the four servant songs (Isa. 42:1-4; 49:1-6; 50:4-11; 52:13–53:12), found in Isaiah 42, has throughout the years been understood by the Christian community as being one that identifies Jesus as the favored one of God who is to bring the fullness of God's justice and salvation to a world living in darkness. Psalm 29 speaks of the sovereignty and self-manifestation of God. The emphasis on the Lordship of God invites the hearer to both affirm God's divinity and God's merciful and very real presence among the people. God is able and is also determined to "bless the people with peace!" The passage from Acts speaks of the lived experience of the early disciples who met at the home of Cornelius with Peter, who have come to know through the life, crucifixion, and resurrection of Jesus, that he is the bearer of God's Spirit and God's promise. Through the Gospel lesson for the day we hear God's own voice proclaiming that Jesus is the Beloved One through whom God will act. Several themes seem to link the passages together: water, the voice of God, the abiding of God's Spirit, and obedience to God.

Certainly the choice of the Twenty-ninth Psalm for use on this day in all three years of the lectionary cycle is in part due to its wonderful imagery of water—a key symbol of baptism. The Lord who is over the waters, in the thunders, and enthroned over the floods, is the power in creation worthy of praise. The one who comes to the River Jordan also transcends the waters of baptism and is worthy of praise.

Matthew 3:17 echoes the words of Isaiah 42:1 as God's own voice declares that Jesus is the beloved servant through whom God's will shall be executed. The sevenfold reference to "the voice of the LORD" in Psalm 29 seems to be an effort to demonstrate to the reader that God's voice can be heard in powerful and majestic, yet known, ways. Thus the revelation of the chosen Servant can be known in listening to God's own voice.

The abiding of God's Spirit is a theme that runs through the passages from Isaiah, Acts, and Matthew. The prophecy of Isaiah announces that the Spirit is upon the chosen Servant. Matthew depicts the abiding of the Spirit through the beautiful and delicate image of a dove descending upon Jesus. In Acts, it is the Spirit of God that breaks down the barriers between Jew and Gentile, demonstrating the universal nature of God's salvation; the same Spirit that Peter proclaims, "God annointed Jesus of Nazareth with" (Acts 10:38).

Finally, there is the theme of obedience to God. The Servant is faithful to the One who is the Lord of all. With this chosen Servant, all of Israel is called to obedience to the Lord who gives breath to the people and stands above all gods. Touched by Jesus, Peter could do no less than obediently preach and testify that Jesus "is the one ordained by God as judge of the living and the dead" (Acts 10:42). Jesus himself, though without sin, is baptized so that all righteousness might be fulfilled in obedience to God's will and plan.

A SERMON BRIEF

While sitting at a favorite window, I watched as the snow came down and wondered when fall had departed and winter had arrived. Some of the snow was beginning to pile up around the trees but most melted when it hit the warmth of the pavement, causing a shiny downhill stream of water. I remembered winters past; the first time I saw snow—a cozy memory before a fireplace, the heady smell of wet pines. How unexpectedly winter had come, but how faithfully it had arrived just as it did every year. I thanked God for winter, experiencing God's presence in the cold wetness.

The psalmist is so right. God is to be seen and heard through creation— through the brightness of winter's first snowflakes, through the mighty rivers and floods that they become, and the cedars that they water; in the flames of fire and the winds that blow powerfully through the oaks leaving forests bare. In all of creation God can be found. Watching the snow fall and meditating on the constancy of God's presence through nature I wondered how one could ever doubt that the Lord is present giving us strength and peace.

There are moments when one does doubt, though. Moments of deep despair when God seems to be silent and absent. The death of a child, the end of a marriage, the news of grave illness, the loss of the job that is one's entire livelihood, are all moments that often bring doubt. For Israel there was doubt in the experience of exile. They had been conquered, dispersed, and enslaved. Israel felt abandoned and alone. The Word of faith is that, especially in moments of human doubt and vulnerability, God is present.

And so the voice came. The voice of the Lord saying, "See, the former things have come to pass, and new things I now declare; before they spring forth, I tell you of them" (Isa. 42:9). Even as Israel struggles, God is preparing her salvation. History tells us that God used the Assyrian King Cyrus to free Israel from her bondage, but God had more in mind than the freedom of a moment in history. So while freeing Israel for the immediate moment, God proclaims that there is more, for God is sending the chosen Servant, the One upon whom God's Spirit rests, to bring eternal justice to the nations. That Servant is Jesus of Nazareth, the very incarnation of God who is always and mercifully present in life.

A beautiful, courageous woman I had the blessing of pastoring helped me to understand how God is present in our lives, always speaking to us and reaching out to us. She had grown up the eldest child in a family of three children. Her mother was an alcoholic and unmarried. All three of the children were fathered by different men, none of whom had ever stayed to help with the family.

Married at sixteen, the woman acquired a husband who was also an alcoholic and who beat her. When the husband died in an automobile accident caused by his drunkenness, the woman entered into a relationship with a married man in exchange for his financial support for her and her children. Her life was fast, confusing, and without future. But one day God's mercy came her way.

She met a man who wanted to marry her. He was attempting to get his life in order and had begun to attend church. At one point he even brought his pastor to visit with her. The woman felt no love for this man and refused to marry him. To her surprise, his care for her and her children did not diminish. The man helped the woman care for the children and their education without asking for anything in return. In a time of particular struggle, the man even had her children live with him so they could complete their school year without interruption. When the woman asked him why he would do such a thing, the man responded by simply saying that it was the Christian thing to do. Gradually the woman began to fall in love with the man and married him. She became a different person. But God had more for her.

Eventually the woman herself came to know the love of Christ and she too began to walk the walk of faith. One day her teenaged son leaned over to me as we watched his mother lead a church meeting and said, "If you had known my mother before you would not have recognized her."

"Yes," she would later affirm, "I am a different person because God was faithful and never forgot me."

Do not doubt. God does not forget. God is as constant as the seasons, more powerful than anything that exists, enthroned as a king forever, yet present with the people giving them strength and peace. God often uses persons to reach out to us but then God completes the divine act of mercy in our lives by sending us Jesus, God's beloved and our Savior.

The woman from my parish sometimes marveled aloud about how Jesus the Son of God could have accepted her, "sinner of sinners." John the Baptist must have experienced some of this inner questioning when Jesus came to him and asked John for baptism. In Matthew 3:15 John states "I need to be baptized by you, and do you come to me?" John is right; Jesus who is without sin needs no baptism. But it is through the act of baptism that Jesus' ministry is inaugurated—the ministry given precisely for the sake of this woman and for John and for each one of us. Our salvation is the fulfillment of God's righteousness as we are washed of our sin and redeemed for God's good work.

And so Jesus was baptized to fulfill the ancient prophecy, "Here is my servant, whom I uphold, my chosen, in whom my soul delights; I have put my spirit upon him; he will bring forth justice to the nations" (Isa. 42:1). Jesus' baptism manifests the eternal faithfulness of God. But Jesus' baptism also calls us to the newness of life that he gives. John the Baptist preached it well, baptizing those who would repent of their sins. Like the woman in my congregation, we must be different—different in the likeness of Jesus who lived righteousness, opened the eyes of the blind, brought the prisoners from the dungeon, and gave light to those who sat in darkness. Through it all, God's constant faithfulness will be with us as sure as the coming of the seasons of God's creation.

SUGGESTIONS FOR WORSHIP

Baptismal Litany (responsive)

LEADER: Remember your baptism and be glad!

PEOPLE: **The waters of God's mercy have flowed and we have been cleansed and refreshed.**

LEADER: Remember the waters that God gathered together and called seas, the mothers of rivers, lakes, and springs that quench the thirst of the earth and all its inhabitants.

PEOPLE: **We drink of the water of God's creation and praise God's name for life.**

LEADER: Remember the waters of the Red Sea and God's salvation.

PEOPLE: **With the people of old, we have been freed from our oppression and brought to a new land.**

LEADER: Remember the well where our Samaritan sister found Jesus and received her blessing.

PEOPLE: **We know that sacred place, for Jesus has also encountered us there; speaking truth to us and yet loving us.**

LEADER: Remember Jesus at the River Jordan; the One who was without sin took upon himself our sin.

PEOPLE: **We are redeemed by Jesus, called to live his righteousness. May God be our help.**

LEADER: Remember God's grace; we are redeemed by Jesus and not by who we are or what we do.

PEOPLE: **Thanks be to God for unmerited grace!**

LEADER: Remember your baptism and be glad!

PEOPLE: **We remember and our lives are filled with joy!**

Fourth Sunday After the Epiphany (Ordinary Time 4)

Mary Donovan Turner

Micah 6:1-8: The people of God are on trial. Again they have disappointed Yahweh. A single worshiper passionately asks the question, "With what shall I come before the Lord?"

Psalm 15: The psalmist tells us who abides with Yahweh. It is they who walk blamelessly, speak truth, do not slander, do not do evil to friends. These qualities form a firm foundation. Those who possess them shall never be moved.

1 Corinthians 1:1-21: God chose the foolish to shame the wise. In this introduction to the letter to the church at Corinth, the writer greets the community and offers them a word of peace. He acknowledges their strength and calls them from their divisions to unity. God has decided through the foolishness of our proclamation to save those who believe.

Matthew 5:1-12: The Sermon on the Mount; the Beatitudes. Jesus, seating the crowds, goes up the mountain. He sits down and speaks to his disciples. "Blessed are. . . ."

REFLECTIONS

In Micah 6:1-5 the prophet uses the image of the court of law to set the stage for a picture of a God disappointed in God's people. Yahweh recounts the stories of old; Yahweh reminds the people of the many ways they have been sheltered, guided, and nurtured by their God through the leaders God had provided for them—Moses, Aaron, and Miriam.

It is the mention of Miriam's name that is shocking to the reader. We would expect Yahweh to remind the community that Moses had been sent to lead them. And Aaron, of course, the brother who was sent to support him. But Miriam? Miriam was the sister who stood by and watched the infant Moses as he lay precariously exposed and vulnerable in the basket in the river. And it was also Miriam who would, after the crossing of the Red Sea, sing a glorious song of victory. But it was also Miriam who would stand outside the camp stricken with leprosy because she had dared to ask a question— Couldn't she, along with her brother, be a spokesperson for Yahweh? Stricken, she stood alienated and isolated from the community. But now, centuries later, she is remembered as a gift given to the people of God.

From the scene of the indicted community standing before God, the edited text moves and sharpens and narrows its focus on a single worshiper. Frustrated by the continual and overwhelming demands of Yahweh, the worshiper passionately asks in essence, "What do you want from me?" The worshiper offers to bring countless gifts to Yahweh. But the prophet reminds the worshiper that she already knows what God requires. Yahweh requires that we act justly, that we love kindness, and that we walk humbly with our God.

A SERMON BRIEF

It is not the kind of silence that sweeps across a worshiping community when they know that they have been touched and bound together by God's spirit.

It's not the kind of hush that comes across a line of students at Pacific School of Religion when they're standing at the edge of the campus at sunset, looking out at the sky blazing with pinks and oranges, as they watch that sun drop into the sea behind the Golden Gate Bridge.

And it's not the kind of silence that we experience when there is a foot or two of snow outside and the world is, if only for a few hours, very quiet.

These kinds of silences are born from knowing beauty and God's spirit and goodness and truth and peace. The kind of silence we experience when we read Micah 6 is not that kind of silence. It's the kind of silence we feel in a courtroom, a silence born out of the world having gone awry. It's the kind of silence that comes from a world that knows pain and sadness, anger and despair.

The judge enters the courtroom and takes her place on the bench. There is a silence as the court is called into session. The defendant rises, feeling, I am sure, as if the whole world is looking upon her. The eyes of the whole world are piercing her back. She is called into accountability for something she has done. She stands there alone. In silence.

In Micah, it is the community of Israel who is standing there in the silent courtroom. God brings the accusation. It is God who has been hurt, and there is this rush of rhetoric; passionate words that come from the mouth of God. What did I do to you? Answer me!!! God bursts into the silence—What did I do to you that you would do this to me? Don't you remember how I traveled with you? I walked with you from Egypt through the Red Sea, through the wilderness to the land of promise? Don't you remember how I have always nestled you in the palm of my hand? Don't you remember those enemies out there in the desert, and how it was me, it was ME who led you through to the land so safely. I loved you. I walked with you so that you would know what kind of God I am, so that you would know salvation. I can almost see tears in God's eyes. The people have now chosen not to walk with God, not to love the God who had saved them. God's speech comes to an end and there's that eerie silence.

The people stand there shuffling their feet. They know its true. They know they have done it again. They have stood in this same courtroom before. How could they have forgotten the agony of their God? And they're wondering, "When did we turn away?" They stand there in that silence.

Finally one of them cries out, What do you want from me? What can I do? What should I do? If I came and bowed down before you, would that be enough? Should I bring an offering to you? I would do that. I will bring the right gift, not just an ordinary gift. I will bring a wonderful gift. A greater gift than any other—thousands of rams into the temple; thousands of rivers of oil. No one has ever brought a gift that large. Not enough? I will give you my child. What do you want from me?

The outburst is answered by the prophet Micah who is standing nearby. He puts his arm on the shoulder of that one who has spoken with such frustration to God. He puts his arm on his shoulder and says to him quietly, You already know. God wants you to walk with God, love like God, and do justice.

I wonder if that worshiper felt any relief at all. Now he knew just exactly what God wanted. No more making wild and rash and lavish promises. No more making futile trips to the altar with gifts that are intended to delight but only offend God. No more spending time and energy on finding the biggest and the best. No more. Just walk. Love. Do justice. Perhaps he wasn't relieved at all, but confused. Very confused. What does it mean to do justice?

His confusion would be ours if Micah had not left us a little clue. At first hidden from us, there is a little clue, a little secret in the middle of God's speech to the people standing in the courtroom. Sometimes people read this story and they don't even know it is there. God is standing in that courtroom, recounting all the wonderful things God has done for God's people. Do you remember those words God spoke in that courtroom? I walked with you from Egypt. I kept you safe. I gave you Moses to lead you. Yes, the people would have nodded their heads; Moses had led their ancestors through that wilderness. And, God said, I gave you Aaron. Yes, the people would have nodded their heads; Aaron had been the support for Moses as he led the people through the wilderness. And, God said, I gave you Miriam. The people of God would be puzzled. Miriam? The Miriam who dared to speak out against her brother Moses? Miriam who thought God could speak through her also, so she spoke? The Miriam who was then stricken with leprosy and who was sent for seven days to stand outside the camp to bear her shame? That Miriam?

God says, Yes! I sent you Moses and Aaron and Miriam. In that simple sentence, at last Miriam has been accorded her rightful place. Her gifts that were once ignored, repressed, silenced, punished, are now acknowledged by her God. GOD WAS DOING JUSTICE! The kind of justice that will reign on this earth when everyone of every race, every gender, every orientation will be recognized as good and valuable and gifted in the eyes of God. That kind of justice, Micah says, that is what God wants.

Do justice. It is as if God is saying, The next time Mother's Day rolls around, don't go and buy me expensive presents and grand gifts. Don't send me a present wrapped up with gold, shiny ribbon. Don't send me dozens of roses. Don't. Just sit down with me at the table, share a meal. Invite my children. All of your brothers and sisters. Invite them to eat with us. That is all I want from you.

When that happens, there will be in this world a great silence. A silence that comes from the beauty that God's world is as it should be.

SUGGESTIONS FOR WORSHIP

Call to Worship

Come let us worship the God who created us, who loves us, who yearns to walk beside us.

Come let us worship the God who calls us to love as God loves, who yearns for justice upon the face of the earth.

Prayer of Confession (Psalm 15 adapted)

LEADER: God of love and expectation, we come before you this day wondering if you abide with us,

PEOPLE: **Wondering if we abide in you.**

LEADER: Forgive us when we fail to walk beside you,

PEOPLE: **Fail to do what is right.**

LEADER: When we do not speak the truth;

PEOPLE: **When we speak about others in ways that are hurtful;**

LEADER: When we do evil to our friends;

PEOPLE: **Argue with our neighbors;**

LEADER: When we glorify those who do not act righteously;

PEOPLE: **When we do not honor those who walk in your name;**

LEADER: Forgive us when we fail to keep our covenants with you and with others;

PEOPLE: **When we take from others what is theirs and do not work for justice;**

ALL: **Forgive us so that we can once again find ourselves rooted firmly in you.**

Assurance of Pardon

LEADER: Friends, believe the Good News.

PEOPLE: **In Jesus Christ, we are forgiven.**

Offertory Statement

God of compassion, shake us from our complacencies. Startle us into an awareness of the need in your world around us. Amen.

Benediction

And now may the God of Moses, Aaron, and Miriam empower you to speak and give you the courage to embrace all those in the world created in the image of God. Amen.

First Sunday in Lent

Amy Miracle

Genesis 2:15-17; 3:1-7: The selected verses tell the story of Adam and Eve's expulsion from the Garden of Eden. God's warning to Adam and Eve concerning the tree of the knowledge of good and evil is followed by the account of the serpent's arm-twisting and of Adam and Eve's realization of their nakedness.

Psalm 32: "Happy are those whose transgression is forgiven."

Romans 5:12-19: Adam is described as a "type" of Christ. Sin and death came into the world through Adam; grace and life came into the world in Christ.

Matthew 4:1-11: After fasting forty days and nights in the wilderness, Jesus withstands the devil's temptations to 1) turn stones into bread, 2) cast himself down from a pinnacle, and 3) worship the devil.

REFLECTIONS

All four texts deal with issues of temptation and sin. The Old Testament lesson contains selections from the second creation story. The psalm tells the story of one who has confessed and has been healed and forgiven by God. In the selection from Romans, Paul compares and contrasts Adam and Christ, focusing on the issue of sin. Matthew's version of the temptation of Jesus is the final selection.

For me the most powerful of the four readings is the Genesis text. This text, however, poses a unique challenge to women preachers. Perhaps more than any other text, this section of Genesis has, over the centuries, been used against women. A sermon could, of course, address such misinterpretations head-on. Another approach is to demonstrate that the text is focused on other, larger issues. My own belief is that the story is not primarily about the relationship between men and women but rather focuses on the relationship between God and humanity.

That focus is consistent with the other lectionary texts and the liturgical season. This first Sunday in Lent is only four days after Ash Wednesday, a day when we remember that we are creatures separate and distinct from the Creator. The theme of our creatureliness continues into the first Sunday in Lent.

I deliberately did not use the word "fall" in the sermon, but instead chose to focus on the question: What went wrong in the garden?

A SERMON BRIEF

I have never had much time for Adam and Eve. It seemed to me as though this story was always being used to make a point—a point about the weakness of women or the sanctity of marriage or the priority of men or humanity's right to be top dog in creation. About a year ago, I reread the story and much to my surprise I found that I loved it. It is a wonderful tale, told by a master storyteller. This morning I want to ask only one question of this text: What went wrong in the garden?

To understand what went wrong in the garden, we must first try to imagine the garden itself. It was a world of utter graciousness and freedom—a garden filled with good things—flowing rivers, plants, animals, a loving creator. In Eden, God gave the humans *good* work to do—to till and keep the garden. But then there were those trees—the tree of life and the tree of the knowledge of good and evil. The reader is not told why the trees were there. One might wish for a garden without such mysterious trees.

God said "You may freely eat of every tree in the garden; but of the tree of the knowledge of good and evil you shall not eat, for in the day that you eat of it you shall die."

Now, let's imagine that you are a guest in someone's home and she or he tells you "Help yourself to any food in the house, feel free to root through the cupboards, the pantry, the refrigerator. My house is your house, except for one thing. In the refrigerator, there is a pink Tupperware container on the second shelf in the back, behind the low-cal mayonnaise—Don't even think of eating what is in there. If you eat it, you will die."

Don't you think at that point you might ask a few questions—What's in the pink Tupperware container? Why keep something so dangerous in your refrigerator?

I believe that Adam showed an amazing lack of curiosity. He asked no questions and no explanation was given as to why the tree was to be avoided. But the prohibition was unambiguous—this was God's world and God set the rules.

Enter the serpent. The serpent was, indeed, more crafty than any other wild animal the Lord God had made. He said that if they were to eat the fruit "you will be like God." He took a clear prohibition and turned it into an "option." God was turned from a loving creator into a rule maker to be circumvented.

The woman and the man ate the fruit. And the world has never been the same.

What exactly did they do wrong? What was the sin of the garden? Was it simple disobedience? Or perhaps a quest for knowledge taken too far? For me the key is found in the words of the serpent—eat the fruit and *you will be like God.*

If you eat the fruit, you will be independent, able to make your own decisions about what to eat and what to believe. If you eat the fruit, you will be your own man and your own woman. Adam and Eve saw a chance for power and autonomy and they grabbed it.

I shouldn't judge them too harshly. That is where I live most of my life—right there, munching on my apple. Every day I profess that Jesus Christ is Lord and then act as if *I* am.

I live much of my life trying to be like God—autonomous, in control, master of my domain, author of my future. I forget every day that the air I breath, the food I eat, the friends I treasure, the job that brings me so much joy are all gifts from God. I take God and God's gifts for granted and then go and take my role in the world far too seriously. I struggle to relinquish the title of the-one-responsible-for-the-well-being-of-the-universe.

Part of me believes that I could usher in the kingdom of God if only I was a little better organized, worked harder, or had a better filing system. In that sense, I am a true Presbyterian.

This may sound like an admirable quality, but it is not; it is arrogance plain and simple. According to the book of Genesis, it is sin.

And it doesn't work. Just ask Adam and Eve—they touched the fruit, they ate the fruit and did they become like God? No, they were naked and afraid. When God called out to them, Adam was ready with his excuse. Adam, who was standing next to Eve the whole time, said "She made me do it." Eve was no better, blaming the serpent for her actions.

Harmony and joy and intimacy were replaced by fear and anxiety. I would suggest that whenever we try to be like God, that is the result. We are simply not cut out for the job. But I can say for myself, I seem to be constantly auditioning for the part.

Several years ago, I presided over a wedding of two church members. We had worked hard to develop a beautiful and meaningful service. The day of the wedding came. As I was driving to the church, I thought to myself, "I wonder if they realize just how *good* I am at weddings. I wonder if they realize how skilled and poised I am—in fact, nothing could happen in a service that would break my composure." Hmm.

Well, the wedding was underway and I had just finished my carefully crafted homily, when one of the men in the wedding party fainted. He did not faint gracefully; he crashed face first into the floor. We got him sitting down in a chair and he seemed to be all right. *Not to worry. I had everything under control.* I had the wedding party do some deep knee bends and the service went on. *Not to worry. I had everything under control.* The time came for the ring bearer to bring us the ring. He took one look at his father, the man who had fainted, and ran out of the sanctuary. *Not to worry. I had everything under control.* I was about half way through the prayer of blessing when I heard the strangest sound. I looked up in time to see one of the flower girls throwing up not two feet away from me.

I stopped midsentence, midprayer, and I started to laugh. The bride and groom started to laugh. In fact, everyone (except for the flower girl) was laughing.

What does it mean to live in a world created by God? It is to joyfully let go of the illusion that we are in control; at the end of the day to foolishly obey a God we will never fully understand. *If* we do that, *when* we do that, we catch a glimpse of something that looks like paradise. Amen.

SUGGESTIONS FOR WORSHIP

Call to Worship (based on Psalm 32)

LEADER: Steadfast love surrounds those who trust in the Lord.

PEOPLE: Be glad in the Lord and rejoice! Shout for joy!

LEADER: The Lord is a hiding place. In times of distress, the rush of mighty waters shall not reach you.

PEOPLE: Be glad in the Lord and rejoice! Shout for joy!

LEADER: The Lord will preserve you from trouble.

PEOPLE: Be glad in the Lord and rejoice! Shout for joy!

Prayer of Confession (in unison)

Catch me in my anxious scurrying, Lord,
and hold me in this Lenten season:
hold my feet to the fire of your grace
and make me attentive to my mortality
    that I may begin to die now
    to those things that keep me
      from living with you
      and with my neighbors on this earth;
    to grudges and indifference,
      to certainties that smother possibilities,
      to my fascination with false securities,
        to my addiction to sweatless dreams,
        to my arrogant insistence on how it has to be;
    to my corrosive fear of dying someday
      which eats away the wonder of living this day,
      and the adventure of losing my life
        in order to find it in you.
Lord, forgive, us.

Assurance of Pardon (in unison)

Because of Jesus Christ, we know that God loves us and will never let us go. Our future is full of hope. In Jesus Christ, we are forgiven.

Benediction

During this season of Lent, may you find time enough for prayer and reflection, time enough to spend with our mysterious and wonderful Lord. May that same Lord bless and keep you always.

Second Sunday in Lent

Jean Alexander

> **Genesis 12:1-4*a*:** Abram is called to leave his father's house and is promised that God will make of him a great nation.
>
> **Psalm 121:** A song celebrating God's protection: "I lift up my eyes to the hills—from whence will my help come?"
>
> **Romans 4:1-5, 14-17:** Abraham's faith is "reckoned to him" as righteousness. God's promise depends on such faith and is guaranteed to all who share it.
>
> **John 3:1-17:** The lecture Jesus gave Nicodemus is recounted: in order to enter the kingdom of God one must be born from above.

REFLECTIONS

This Gospel text gave rise to several questions. Who was Nicodemus and how might he be like the people in my congregation? What was his motivation for coming to see Jesus "by night"? How can I rescue the charge to be "born again" for my mainline congregation—some of whom relate the phrase to all they dislike and fear about evangelical or fundamentalist Christianity? How can I help them hear what Jesus is asking?

I found that focusing on who the Pharisees were was a helpful place to begin. We often see the Pharisees as the enemy. However, according to biblical scholarship, they were more like mainline Protestants. They were concerned with doing good and obeying the law. From there it was not hard to compose a picture of Nicodemus that was recognizable to the people of my congregation of this kind of character. Frederick Buechner's treatment of biblical characters in *Peculiar Treasures* provides an example of and inspiration for this kind of character sketch. I find that once I begin to do an empathetic treatment of a person, like Nicodemus, the rest of the sermon often falls into place. If I can identify with who he might have been, then I can understand what might have motivated him to seek Jesus out.

Working with some good commentaries, I was helped to see how ambiguous and deliberately challenging Jesus' words to Nicodemus were. In addition, the double meaning of the Greek word *anothen* reminds us of the spiritual nature of John's Gospel. It highlights the struggle between the literal self that wants programs and concrete answers and the spiritual self that must be open and trusting, like an infant.

Again, I found it helpful to imagine the condition of infancy and all that it evokes. For, as a woman, it is a powerful image and reminds me of my own experiences as a mother. In a time when many men have also had experiences with their children's birth and nurture, it is a strong and useful image for the congregation of how the spiritual life must begin.

A SERMON BRIEF

There was once a young girl named Alice, famous for her curiosity. She ended up in Wonderland because of it. She fell down a rabbit hole, had tea with the Mad Hatter, and met a cat with a smile that wouldn't disappear, even though he did. These were just a few of the things that happened to her.

Curiosity is the desire to know why things are the way they are. It is a quality of human life, however, that we are decidedly ambivalent about. We say "curiosity killed the cat" to indicate that the desire to know things can get us into trouble. In Greek mythology, a girl named Pandora was responsible for letting all the troubles of life out of the box because of her curiosity.

I'm not sure I accept the cultural premise that women are more curious than men. I think that curiosity is a human quality. Without curiosity, how would we ever learn? It is wonderful when our children want to know about the world. Their curiosity is a gift to be treasured and encouraged.

Do you remember being curious as a child? Did you wonder about storms? Did you sneak through your mother's drawers to see what was there? Were you curious about the difference between boys and girls? Did you wonder about God? I hope so.

What are you curious about now? What is it that you wonder about? Do you secretly read the tabloids in the supermarket checkout line? Are you fascinated with the lifestyles of the rich and famous? Are you curious about the latest discoveries about space or medicine? Are you a political junkie with a need to absorb all the details of the latest presidential campaign? Are you ever curious about life itself? About why you are here? About the meaning of your life? If you are, then perhaps you can understand why Nicodemus, this highly respected leader of the Pharisees, sought Jesus out by night.

Nicodemus had it all. He was a partner in his Jerusalem law firm. He had a nice house in the suburbs with a Jacuzzi in the master bath. He had a good wife and two high achieving children. He was a pillar of the congregation and a leader in the PTA. He had never caused his parents any grief to speak of. And yet Nicodemus was aware, as he drove his Lexus to work every day, that something was missing. There were times, in the middle of the night, or in a particularly boring meeting with some corporation, that he found himself wondering if this was all there was to life.

Yes, Nicodemus was like a lot of middle-class folks today. He had worked hard. He had played by the rules. He had achieved a measure of security professionally and financially. He had done all the right things, jumped through all the right hoops. He got up every day and was responsible. And yet he was aware of wondering what the purpose of all of this was. Sometimes he sat in worship and wondered if he even believed in anything anymore.

There were times it occurred to him that maybe he ought to talk to someone about this. But who? Everyone else seemed to be into the program. No one else seemed to have any questions about the meaning of all this stuff we call life. Surely he couldn't talk to the pastor? She seemed so sure of her belief. Or his law partners? They might think he was having a midlife crisis and about to run off with that attractive new secretary.

There WAS someone he would like to ask about all this. There was this man named Jesus that everyone was talking about. Ever since the Feast of the Tabernacles, Jerusalem had been buzzing about how Jesus had gone into the Temple and overturned the tables of the money changers and those who sold the animals and birds for sacrifice. Some said he could turn water into wine. Now there was a power Nicodemus wouldn't mind having, given the cost of a good chardonnay these days.

No wonder Nick sought Jesus out by night. It wouldn't do for others to see him talking with this controversial figure. It wouldn't do for it to get around that he had been seen with this religious nut. People would think he was crazy and it wouldn't do to get that reputation when you were a respected community leader.

Eventually of course, we know Nick's curious hunger overcame his fear. He went out to meet Jesus face-to-face—albeit under the cover of night. It was a curious meeting. As John tells it, it was not an easy conversation they had. Nick and Jesus didn't seem to communicate very well. For a smart man, Nick seemed positively obtuse.

Nick spoke first. But instead of coming right out with his questions, he began by saying, "Well, Jesus, we know you are a teacher about God and must have some great spiritual powers. I guess you must be from God since it isn't likely that anyone could do what you do and not be from God." You almost want to scream, "Hey, Nick! What is on your mind? Out with it!" And even though he couldn't quite come out and ask Jesus what he wanted to know, Jesus answered him. "Nick, the truth is that you won't see God's realm unless you are born again."

Now we need to take a time-out here before going on. For some people here this phrase "born again" is a real turnoff, so we need to stop and ask, "What is really being said here?" You may have noticed that the NRSV did not say "born again" but "born from above." This is not an accident, nor a whim of the liberal translators. The Greek word *anothen*, which means "to be born," is a word that has a double meaning. It means both a time of birth, "again" and the place from which that birth originates, "from above." Not only that but this word *anothen* is paired with the phrase "the realm of God," which also has two dimensions. The realm or kingdom of God is both a place where God rules and the time of God's reign. For a literal-minded person like Nick, it is as if Jesus is speaking gibberish.

"How can anyone be born after having grown old? Can one enter a second time into the mother's womb and be born?" There is almost a sarcastic edge to Nick's question. It is the question of someone who cannot see beyond the surface of life. It is the question of someone who wants a program, a list of seven habits of highly effective people, a concrete way to rid himself of these questions that are keeping him awake at three A.M.

This is a problem that WE have with the Gospel of John. We come to this Gospel wanting a history of Jesus, or at least a set of rules to follow. Instead, what we get are these long stories full of images and symbolism. We get symbolic truth about the nature of God and Christ. We ask Jesus a question that we think is perfectly logical and he answers another question.

Nicodemus wanted to know who Jesus was. Jesus didn't answer his question. Instead, Jesus told Nick what had to happen to him before he could begin to understand the questions that were troubling his life. Before he could understand who Jesus was, he had to learn a new way of seeing. Jesus seemingly said, "You aren't going to get answers to your question, Nick, until you get a spiritual rebirth. You aren't going to solve your restless heart until you let go and let the spirit make you like a newborn baby; vulnerable, trusting, dependent, and hungering for the food that only God can give."

There is the rub. There is the stumbling block that trips us up every time. For who of us wants to place ourselves back in such a relationship of radical dependency such as we had in infancy? Who of us wants to be as vulnerable as we were as a nursing infant? No, we have fought too hard for our independence and security to want to give it up. Even when Jesus goes on to tell us of God's trust and vulnerability, we are afraid. Jesus tells us that God's love for the world is so great that God risked sending him, his only child, to live among us so that we might be renewed in love and faith. In retrospect, it was a tremendous risk, given how Jesus was received.

So where does this leave us? Where does it leave Nicodemus? The story doesn't really have an end. It is left open-ended. We are left not with the question that Nicodemus asked Jesus, but with the question of how we are going to respond to the invitation Jesus makes to us. Jesus says, "open up your life to the spirit of God. Open up your heart to the wonder of rebirth. Admit to the deep hunger that is within you, and be fed by my spirit. Come, not by night, but by day, trusting that God will feed you."

SUGGESTIONS FOR WORSHIP

Call to Worship (John 3:16)

LEADER: God so loved the world

PEOPLE: That [God] gave [the] only Son,

LEADER: So that everyone who believes in [God]

PEOPLE: May not perish but may have eternal life.

Prayer of Confession

Eternal God, whose Word is a lamp for our feet and a light for our path, we confess that we have failed to respond fully to your gracious presence in our lives. Through Jesus Christ you have offered us new life, fulfillment, and the freedom to serve you. We confess that we are captive to sin, that our sins bind us with false pride, and that the wrong we do is made worse by the good we leave undone. Reconcile us to you and to all people. God of mercy, forgive all our sin and strengthen us anew for life as you intend it. Through Jesus Christ, our Savior. Amen.

Words of Assurance

God hears the confession of our hearts and lips. Through Jesus we are forgiven all our sins, and by the Holy Spirit we are empowered for new life. Thanks be to God!

Benediction (Ps. 121 adapted)

Your foot shall not stumble
The sun shall not strike you
All evil shall be kept from your door
For the God who made heaven and earth is your help.
And God will keep your going out and your coming in from this time on and forevermore.

....

Third Sunday in Lent

Joanna Dewey

....

Exodus 17:1-7: During their wilderness journey the Israelites complain bitterly to Moses about their thirst. God directs Moses to strike a rock; he does so and water pours forth.

Psalm 95: This popular call to worship contains references to the Exodus 17 story.

Romans 5:1-11: Since we are justified by faith, we have peace with God. We boast in our hope and also in our sufferings, for Christ died for us while we were still sinners.

John 4:5-42: Jesus meets the Samaritan woman by Jacob's well and engages her in theological discourse.

REFLECTIONS

Last week, we heard about Nicodemus, the high-ranking Jew who came secretly to talk to Jesus at night. Today, in the Gospel reading, we hear about a nameless woman from Sychar, whom Jesus came to talk with, on his way north to Galilee. Actually, it is pretty clear that what you have heard was the Gospel's imaginative recounting of Jesus' meetings with Nicodemus and with me, the Samaritan woman. And today I wish to give you my imaginative recounting of my meeting with Jesus. I make no claims to historical accuracy; I do claim that fiction is often a better revealer of truth.

A Sermon Brief

Last week you heard about naming, and I have no name. That is, you do not know my name; of course I have one. But I don't think I will tell you what it is. You all, Christians through the centuries, have made up so many odd (and some not very nice) things about me that I think I would rather keep my name to myself. You can call me the Samaritan woman—although there were quite a lot of us. But that's the way you often tend to dismiss groups you look down on—the Black women, the Asian women—as if there weren't lots of Black women, and lots of Korean, and Japanese, and Chinese and other Asian women. And besides, Jesus was in Samaria—wouldn't you expect to find Samaritans there?

You can call me the woman at the well! Really, that's like saying, the woman at the grocery store. I was taken on a visit to Star Supermarket yesterday, and I was quite amazed at what I saw. I think I like your grocery stores and water that comes out of a pipe in your house. But back in my day, women went to wells for water; we might have to make a dozen or more trips a day to get water, so there's nothing unusual about a woman at a well. Now some of your people—commentators you call them I think—make a big deal of my being alone at the well. They seem to think I'm an outcast in my village because I was there by myself. And it's true we women mostly go out together in the morning and the evening; it makes the work less burdensome when we can chat and sing together. But still we all go out now and again during the day. Sometimes we—or more likely our kids—knock a jug over; or sometimes we need more water, or sometimes we just want to get away and be alone for a little bit. We trade off and leave our kids with one another or with the older children, and go off alone to the well. The men think we just didn't plan right, and we let them think that, but we know the truth.

So I'm no outcast, the women and the men of the village like me and respect me. Why wouldn't they? My hospitality is generous, and I do my share of the work. Indeed, even in your story, it's clear I'm respected. The people of the village all listen to me when I come back and tell them about Jesus, and they come out after me to see for themselves. They wouldn't do that if I were an outcast. Your commentators aren't very consistent, making me an outcast and then having the village listen to me. I think they're just like the disciples who didn't see why Jesus should talk to a woman.

Your commentators also make a big deal about all my husbands. You seem to think I behaved shamelessly. But I didn't, you know. (Chaucer's wife of Bath—another nameless woman—she and I have had some good talks about this.) But back to my story. Jesus was just showing me he was a prophet—how else could he do this except by telling me about my life. And he didn't imply I was evil or dirty. That's your doing. That's part of why I'm here today, to set my story right. Besides, that was the beginning of our theological discourse—we weren't just talking about me, we were talking about the five gods of Samaria, the gods of my place. To give them credit, some of your commentators do get that right.

I'll come back to our theological discourse, Jesus' and mine, but first I want you to listen to the story you heard read. Just as Peter and Andrew and James and John in your other Gospels left their boats and their nets behind, so I left my water jug. Just as Andrew heard Jesus, and went to get Simon Peter, saying "We have found the Messiah." Just as Philip found Nathanael and said "We have found him about whom Moses in the law and also the prophets wrote," so I went and told all my village about this man, who could be the Messiah. And because of my witness, the whole village came out and met Jesus, and heard for themselves, and came to know that he was indeed the Savior of the World. But first of all it was because of my words that they believed. One of your commentators calls me the first successful missionary. I like that commentator.

But what I really want to talk about today is my discourse with Jesus. For that's the real point, the Good News about the Messiah, the Savior of the World, who brings us living water. I'm just one of many women and many men who have told the world about Jesus. Actually many commentators, even Jesus' male disciples in the story, seem to be struck by the fact that Jesus was even talking to the likes of me, a woman of Samaria. From the Jewish perspective, I'm one of those despicable unclean Samaritans. And from the viewpoint of the Jewish religious leaders, at least, I'm especially unclean because I'm female. But that's to look at my story from *their* perspective. As a Samaritan, I think the Jews, even Jesus sometimes, are funny uptight people concerned with their own specialness before God. (Remember what Jesus said to the Syrophoenician woman about Gentiles being dogs? Now really!) And Jesus is here at *my* well, a Samaritan well. And *he's* quite willing to ask me for water. And this female impurity bit, that's a lot of male hoopla, men's ideas. Men are just as much physical bodies as we women—I know—and I think God created our bodies just as well as theirs were created.

But back to my discussion with Jesus, the real point. (I keep getting led off track by all these extraneous matters that your text and commentators assume is the real point.) The *point* of our discussion is about *where* you worship God. We started talking about whether it is Jerusalem (as the Jews think) or the mountain of Samaria (as we Samaritans believe). And Jesus said the time was coming, indeed is already here, when God is to be worshiped without regard to place, that God could be worshiped anywhere, not just in special religious places. I rather like that odd translation you used today, "God is not tied to place"; to worship God truly is to worship "without regard to place" (AT).

The Greek text reads that to worship God as God truly is, is to worship "in spirit and truth" *en pneumati kai aletheia*. Spirit and truth are sort of cozy religious words, don't you think? I expect the Jews in their Temple, while it stood, thought they were worshiping God in spirit and truth. And I know we Samaritans thought we were, in our holy places. But the Good News of Jesus is that God is not tied to place, that the living water, the fountain of real life, is available to us all everywhere—not just in some particular place, be it Jerusalem, Rome, Constantinople, Canterbury, or this chapel here at the Episcopal Divinity School.

Of course, true worship can and does occur here—I plan to stay and worship with you this morning if I may. But that's not the point. The point is, it doesn't *only* occur here, or even *especially* occur here. It occurs inside and outside of churches, inside and outside of denominations, even outside of what we think of as religion. And neither the Jews nor the Samaritans, nor any of your many different churches has any special claim to worship in more "spirit and truth" than others. God makes the offer of eternal life to us all.

Oh, I was warned, you are all very individualistic now. I'm not saying that worship is just an individual matter. I'm saying that communities worship God, without regard to place, and any attempt to establish a place as a better, or truer or more spiritual place is human pride; humans putting themselves and their institutions in the place of God. The point is that God's living water, the true fountain of life, is offered to us all, and I—oops, I almost told you my name, and I said I wasn't going to do that—a woman of Samaria, invite and exhort you wherever you are to drink deeply of God's living water, to enjoy and rejoice in the satisfying water God gives us.

And I thank you for listening to me this morning.

SUGGESTIONS FOR WORSHIP

Call to Worship

LEADER: Let us make a joyful noise to the rock of our salvation.

PEOPLE: Let us make a joyful noise to God with songs of praise.

LEADER: For God is our rock, who leads us in the wilderness,

PEOPLE: And meets us at the well,

LEADER: Who sustains us in the desert

PEOPLE: And knows our heart's great need.

LEADER: God is our rock, the wellspring of all that is good.

ALL: Come, let us drink deeply, let us worship God.

Call to Confession

Do not harden your hearts as your ancestors did at Meribah.
Do not test the Lord as your forebears did at Massah.
Do not quarrel with God, but turn to the Lord in confidence.
Turn to the Lord, who is ready to meet every need.

Prayer of Confession

We would worship you in Spirit, O God,
but our appetites distract us and
the here-and-now seems to get in the way.
We would worship you in truth, O God,
but our hearts are pulled between loyalties
and our logical minds balk at your words.
Forgive us, we pray, for our doubts and our lusts.
And lead us to your living water
That we may be washed clean of the world's concerns
and cured of our thirst. In the name of Jesus Christ. Amen.

Assurance of Pardon

Since we are justified by faith, we have peace with God through our Lord
Jesus Christ.
Friends, believe the Good News.

Fourth Sunday in Lent

Lucy A. Rose

I Samuel 16:1-13: The prophet Samuel anoints the youngest of Jesse's sons, David, as king.

Psalm 23: The psalmist images God as shepherd and provider.

Ephesians 5:8-14: Using the metaphors of light and waking up, the writer urges believers to live lives pleasing to God as they "rise from the dead" into Christ as shining light.

John 9:1-41: The story of Jesus' healing of the man born blind and Jesus' claim to be the light of the world.

REFLECTIONS

After the ordinariness of ordinary days and before the feasting and festivity of Easter comes Lent—a time-out kind of time. Lent pulls up a rocking chair and says, "Here, sit down. Think about what you've done and what's been done to you. Take your time. See if you can eke out meaning from your yesterdays, todays, and tomorrows." And while we rock, Lent tells us stories so we can lay our lives beside them. "What's going on?" we are invited to ask. "What is God up to in these ancient stories and in our own?"

A SERMON BRIEF

On this fourth Sunday in Lent I invite you to lay the story of the man born blind beside your own life. Take your time, as I probe the intersections between this ancient story and my own battle with cancer.

It was a routine breast exam—granted I hadn't done one in months—but, well, I didn't expect the large mass I felt, and then felt again. A mammogram, a sonogram, and a biopsy confirmed my fears. Ten days later I had a mastectomy. Chemotherapy followed with its tagalongs: nausea, hair loss, and weariness. It was while I was receiving chemotherapy that my companionship began with the man born blind.

Sitting there on the side of the thoroughfare, he listened keenly to the passersby. He could distinguish those who would hurry by from those who might slow up and pause. And he listened to the voices. He stayed up on most current events just by listening to the passing conversations. The footsteps of a small crowd slowed as they approached him. "Rabbi," he heard, "who sinned, this man or his parents, that he was born blind?" (John 9:2). "Does it matter?" he thought, "I'm blind, a blind beggar." The voice that answered with its arresting note of authority claimed his full attention: "Neither this man nor his parents sinned; he was born blind so that God's works might be revealed in him" (John 9:3).

Here was my first point of contact with this first-century story. In the few books that I read about cancer, I found the same question being asked and the disciples' answers assumed. I have cancer. Who sinned? Answer One: I had. I hadn't eaten right, lived right, married right, coped with stress right. I read stories like this one of a woman who, when she got cancer, divorced her husband, quit her job, bought a house in the country, got the dog she'd always wanted, and was enjoying tending her garden. *And* she was cancer free. See, if I just. . . . Clearly my cancer was my own fault. Answer Two: Our parents sinned. Other authors insist that cancer is caused by toxic foods, toxic water, toxic air, toxic toothpaste. It is past generations who have polluted the environment, and we are merely reaping the havoc they wreaked.

Jesus' answer came as a word of good news to me. No one sinned. Or rather, maybe we're all at fault, but why ask? I did not find the standard answers especially helpful, and certainly not healing. Rather, what Jesus offered was a way to rethink my story: I have cancer "so that God's works might be revealed" in me (John 9:3). I believed this four-and-a-half years ago during my first bout with cancer, and I believe it now that the cancer has reappeared in my bones: My cancer—wherever it came from—is an opportunity for God's works to be revealed in me.

My companionship with the man born blind continued. After the man was healed, the text has him recount his story three times—a long version with vivid details, a middling version, and, shortest of all, "I was blind, now I see" (John 9:25). Such repetition is surprising in the biblical literature. Clearly his telling of the handiwork of God in his life is important, for thereby he confirms the words of Jesus: God's work had been revealed in him. For me the story was an invitation to discern God's handiwork in my own life and to declare God's works to others.

There have been many moments of grace in my battle with cancer. While I and my husband waited to see the surgeon before the mastectomy, a hymn floated into my consciousness and I began to sing it over and over again to myself:

> Have thine own way, Lord! Have thine own way!
> Thou art the potter; I am the clay.
> Mold me and make me after thy will,
> while I am waiting, yielded and still.

Waiting, waiting, waiting. Waiting for the surgeon, waiting for news of the lump, waiting for God, yielded and still and waiting for God. The hymn for me was a gift from God's Holy Spirit.

I had the mastectomy the next day. This time the gift-hymn was different. As I was being wheeled down the hall to the operating room, I began singing—through no deliberate effort on my part:

> The lone, wild bird in lofty flight
> Is still with Thee, nor leaves Thy sight.
> And I am Thine! I rest in Thee.
> Great Spirit, come, and rest in me.

The song was still singing itself inside me as I swam into consciousness in the recovery room. I woke up from the anesthesia singing, "And I am Thine! I rest in Thee. Great Spirit, come, and rest in me."

Two days later, the day I would go home to a household of help, the Spirit gave me a third gift-hymn. Again I woke up singing. This time the words were:

> To God be the glory through Jesus the Son.
> I'll give God the glory, great things God has done.
> Praise to God. Praise to God.
> Let the earth hear your voice.
> Praise to God. Praise to God.
> Let the peoples rejoice.
> To God be the glory through Jesus the Son.
> I'll give God the glory, great things God has done.

I realized later I had adapted and altered the words for inclusivity. What mattered on that postsurgery morning was that I was singing praises to God who had been at work in me, not, as it turned out, eradicating the cancer but postponing it for three years and tuning my heart to sing praises.

Then the two stories turn bleak and ugly. The man, once he could see, gave God the glory and was consequently cast out of the synagogue. He was cut off from his people—his parents, his neighbors, his God. Where were his praises as he weighed the question, Which is better, to be a blind beggar or a castaway who can see and has no place to go? How long did he suffer his cast-out status? How long did he contemplate his dubious gift of sight before Jesus "heard that they had driven him out, and . . . found him"? (John 9:35). How long? A few hours? A few days? But Jesus *did* find him and reawakened, even deepened, his faith. The story says the man—still cast out, still cut off, still unsure of his tomorrows—responded to Jesus with faith and worship. "I believe," he said, and worshiped him (John 9:38).

And me? There were long weeks of chemotherapy when no praises rose to my lips; and even now there are seasons of depression and weakness and tears—tears for my seven-year-old daughter whose mother may die before next Christmas, tears for my husband of twelve years, tears for myself when the pain attacks and my energy sags and I feel useless, and tears for all those who suffer from illness and grief, torture and abuse, hopelessness and the fear of death. And yet, from time to time, God in Jesus still seeks me out and shores up my faith through a dream, a card, a prayer, a phone call, the touch of a loved one, the gift of food or a book, or countless, countless other reminders of the grace-filled handiwork of God. When I am strong, I am thankful that, however unsure I am of my tomorrows, however imminent my death may be, I can still, by God's Spirit at work in me, believe and worship—and on most days, that is enough.

Thanks be to God for Lent's gift of reflective time, for biblical stories that tease meaning from our own stories, and for the unfailing workings of God in Jesus Christ, through whom we believe and whose praises we declare through our worship and our recounting of God's handiwork in our lives.

SUGGESTIONS FOR WORSHIP

Call to Worship (Eph. 5:14)

LEADER: "Sleeper, awake! Rise from the dead, and Christ will shine on you."

PEOPLE: **"Sleeper, awake! Rise from the dead, and Christ will shine on you."**

Prayer of Confession

God, our Shepherd and Guide, forgive us when we turn from you and your provident care. Forgive us when we forget your rod and staff and panic in the face of death and its shadows—loss, disappointment, and those times when life careens out of control. Forgive our complaining, our inability to discern your activity in our lives, our reluctance to follow Jesus on the journey to the cross. Turn us back, O God, to yourself; accompany us as we face life's twists and turns; and open our eyes to your workings in our lives that we may praise you and speak of your faithfulness to others.

Charge and Benediction (Eph. 5:8*b*-10, 14)

"Live as children of light—for the fruit of the light is found in all that is good and right and true. Try to find out what is pleasing to the Lord." And may Christ shine upon you, awakening you from sleep and raising you to new life.

Easter Day

Cynthia Hale

Acts 10:34-43: Peter preaches to Cornelius and his household.

Jeremiah 31:1-6: God promises to be faithful, and the prophet foresees that the people's response will be dancing, merrymaking, and harvesttime joy.

Psalm 118:1-2, 14-24: The congregation is encouraged to give thanks for God's goodness and steadfast love. The psalmist praises God— "my strength," "my might," and "my salvation"—for life after the threat of death, for an answer to prayer, for "the day that the LORD has made."

Colossians 3:1-4: The writer declares that we have died and been raised with Christ. Therefore our thoughts should be on things above as we hope in Christ.

John 20:1-18: One account of the women's visit to the tomb on Easter morning and Jesus' commissioning of Mary Magdalene.

Matthew 28:1-10: Another account of the women's visit to the tomb and their carrying news of Jesus' resurrection to the disciples.

REFLECTIONS

In the history of the world, only one tomb has ever had a rock rolled before it, a Roman seal placed on it, and soldiers stationed in front of it to prevent the dead from rising. That was the tomb of Christ Jesus.

I remember Anwar Sadat's body lying in state in Cairo, John Kennedy's body in Washington, and Martin Luther King Jr.'s in Atlanta. All had military personnel whose presence witnessed to their prominence and ensured the orderly nature of the crowd who passed by to view the body. But, I repeat, only once have armed soldiers been posted to watch the dead.

What could be more ridiculous than guards keeping their eyes on a corpse? But they did!

Now, they knew Jesus was dead! The soldiers had pierced his side to make sure. Pilate had him certified dead before allowing Joseph of Arimathea to take his body. Surely Joseph would not have wrapped the body of Jesus and buried him alive.

They knew he was dead! They had heard him say, "It is finished" (John 19:30) and "Father, into your hands I commend my spirit" (Luke 23:46). They had heard him cry out and die.

But they had also heard him say, "Destroy this temple and in three days I will raise it up" (John 2:19). They had heard him compare himself with Jonah who was in the belly of the whale for three days and so he would be in the belly of the earth for three days (Matt. 12:40).

Would he rise? They didn't think so. Were the chief priests and Pharisees afraid the Lord of life would keep his word? Perhaps they needed to make sure. So they went to see Pilate and received permission to seal the tomb and place guards to keep watch day and night. They made the tomb as secure as they could.

Those guards had an impossible assignment. Little did they know that while they were standing on the outside, God was at work on the inside. God does some of the best work undercover. Without our knowledge, while we sleep, while we worry, as we pray, even before we realize we need divine help, God is taking care of business. While the soldiers were standing on the outside, God was at work on the inside raising Jesus.

A SERMON BRIEF

The followers of Jesus had heard him speak in forbidden symbols, parables, and straightforward speech about the resurrection that would follow his death. It seems they had heard the part about his death. But obviously they had completely missed the part about his resurrection.

It is clear the disciples didn't believe they would ever see Jesus alive again. After his crucifixion they all fled in fear. Now they were living without hope, in despair, hiding behind closed doors, wondering if they would be next. They didn't believe he would rise again. They didn't take him at his word.

Nor did the women believe they would see Jesus alive. In Matthew's Gospel, early Sunday morning just before dawn, Mary Magdalene and the other Mary went to the tomb. They wanted to pay their last respects to their dead friend. Like the disciples they didn't take Jesus at his word.

Isn't that the way it is with us? We don't believe God's word. We don't believe God will do what God promises. If we did, we wouldn't live our lives the way we do—on the edge, barely making it from day to day. God has promised to take care of us. What is it that causes us to distrust God's promises and not believe God's word? Why is it so hard for us to believe God?

Is it because we judge God by our own human standards and actions? As humans, we make promises all the time and forget or fail to keep them. Sometimes we have every intention of keeping them, but something comes up to prevent it. Time and again we get disappointed by persons who say they will but don't, who give us their word and then fail to follow through. Politicians make campaign promises that last only until after the election. Lovers make promises to be faithful until death, when what they really mean is the death of the relationship.

We think that maybe God is like us. But God is not! Others may disappoint us. We may disappoint ourselves and others. But God will never disappoint us. God's ways are higher than our ways. We try, but even the best of us in our human frailty get flaky at times. But God is faithful. God is a God who keeps promises. When God makes a promise, God is obligated by Divine character to perform it. God is a God of truth; God cannot lie.

The women who went to the tomb never expected to see Jesus alive. They were looking for a body to embalm. They were looking for a corpse. But when they got there, they found the stone rolled away and an angel sitting on it. The angel said to the women, "Do not be afraid; I know that you arc looking for Jesus who was crucified. He is not here; for he has been raised, as he said. Come, see the place where he lay" (Matt. 28:5-6).

It's been said that the angel didn't move the stone to let Jesus out, but to let the women in. God knew that even with seeing the stone rolled away the women would not be convinced that Jesus had been raised. They needed proof. Perhaps, if they entered the empty tomb and saw where he had lain, perhaps then they would believe that he was not there but had been raised.

They needed proof, assurance. Notice the angel's words, "as he said." God is a God of kept promises. God always keeps his word. God promised that Jesus, the Holy One, would not see decay and he didn't.

God will do what God promises. Proof? You say you need proof? Faith is what God asks of us. Faith is the assurance of things hoped for, the conviction of things not seen (Heb. 11:1). Faith is believing without seeing. Faith is utter dependence and reliance upon God. Faith says that if God said it, I believe it.

You've tried to trust God, but God is too slow? One cannot determine when God will keep promises. God cannot be rushed. God promised Abraham and Sarah a baby, but it was years before Isaac was born. God promised David he would be King of Israel but he remained a fugitive for years before he was crowned.

God has promised to provide for your needs. But you're at the end of your rope? Hang on, God is on the way. You're at the end of your resources? Hang on. You're at the end of your patience? Hang on. God won't let you fall.

The angel told the women to go and tell the disciples that Jesus was alive and would appear before them in Galilee. Now, you know that having seen the empty tomb and having heard the angel's announcement, the women were filled with joy. *But* they were also afraid. It was hard for them to believe that Jesus was alive. Their joy mingled with fear; their hope that the angel's words were true mingled with uncertainty.

Sometimes it seems hard to believe that God can do what God promises, especially when the situation looks impossible to us. It will take a miracle to turn the situation around, we say. But let us remember that what seems like a miracle to us is natural for God. Nothing is impossible to God. Raising Jesus from the dead was no miracle for God; it was just keeping God's word. Creating the earth and all that's in it was no miracle for God. It was all in a week's work.

Still you are afraid; you doubt? Perhaps on this Easter Day you may also be filled with joy, like the women who ran to tell the disciples. Matthew says they left the tomb and Jesus met them. On their way, he presented himself to them. As they stepped out on the angel's word, "he has been raised, as he said," they met Jesus. He appeared to them and gave them the assurance that they needed.

As you trust God today and believe God's word, you too will encounter Jesus Christ. God will become real to you as God did to the women. Faith is what makes the resurrection believable. Take hold of God's word. The resurrection of Jesus is proof that God keeps promises. Jesus is risen as he said. He has passed from death to life. He has conquered sin and death. Death could not hold him. And the resurrection of Jesus brings new possibilities for our lives. Try him for yourself.

I tried him for myself one day. I found him to be a friend who sticks closer than any other. I tried him for myself. He has proved himself to me over and over again. He has given me new life and a new perspective. No more am I bound by discouragement and fear. No longer can death have a hold on me. He has given me eternal life. I live each day with a new sense of confidence because I've taken him at his word.

SUGGESTIONS FOR WORSHIP

Call to Worship (Jer. 31:3, 4*b*, 6*b*)

LEADER: God says, "I have loved you with an everlasting love";

PEOPLE: God says, "I have continued my faithfulness to you."

LEADER: Take up your tambourines and go forth in the dance of the merrymakers.

PEOPLE: "Come, let us go up to Zion, to the LORD our God."

Easter Prayer

Faithful God, take away our doubt and renew our faith in the resurrection of Jesus Christ. Take away our fear and grant us resurrection joy, so that we may run to tell others that Jesus lives. Lead us to step out on your promises so that by stepping out we may experience anew the risen presence of Jesus not only today but day after day until you call us home through the final resurrection into eternal life.

Charge and Benediction (Col. 3:1-4)

"If you have been raised with Christ, seek the things that are above, where Christ is, seated at the right hand of God. Set your minds on things that are above, not on things that are on earth, for you have died, and your life is hidden with Christ in God." And may Christ who is your life, keep you faithful until you and all the faithful are revealed with Christ in glory.

Second Sunday of Easter

Barbara Lundblad

Acts 2:14a, 22-32: The second, and less familiar, half of Peter's sermon at Pentecost. Jesus' life, death, and resurrection show him to be the Messiah.

Psalm 16: "The LORD is my chosen portion and my cup." The psalmist declares confidence in God and prays for continuing protection.

I Peter 1:3-9: Through the resurrection of Jesus Christ we have been born anew to a "living hope."

John 20:19-31: After his resurrection, Christ appears to the disciples and then, a week later, to Thomas. Thomas has to be shown the nail prints in Jesus' hands before he will believe.

REFLECTIONS

John's resurrection stories are wondrous in detail: Peter getting beat out on the race to the tomb, the long account of Mary Magdalene looking for Jesus outside the tomb, the first visitation with all the disciples except Thomas and another a week later that included Thomas. The details seem to contradict one another in marvelous ways. "Do not hold on to me," spoken to Mary Magdalene changes to "Put your finger here. . . . Reach out your hand and put it in my side," in the evening. Jesus moves through locked doors as though a spirit, yet Jesus' wounds are bodily enough to be seen and touched. (Whether any of the disciples actually touched him is unclear, but the scars were seen by the disciples, including Thomas.) And three times—like a liturgy—the greeting: "Peace be with you." We see Jesus speaking the word of peace with outstretched arms, the nail prints plainly visible. This peace comes from the resurrected, wounded one. This peace comes in spite of the disciples' fear, in spite of Thomas's doubts, in spite of things not being fixed up. This peace is spoken within our liturgies not as a greeting reserved for our friends, but as the very word of Jesus to those we can't stand, those with whom we disagree, those we would never invite to dinner, even those who have wounded us.

The breath of the Spirit is also from the Wounded One. The Spirit is breathed upon the disciples by Jesus the Crucified; the Spirit doesn't float away from earth but descends upon the children of earth even as the eternal Logos didn't remain a grand design but pitched a tent among us. The focus on the wounds is surely not a new idea, but I wanted people to see that the risen, wounded Christ meets them in the wounds of their own lives (though a preacher could rightly point to the woundedness of the world).

A SERMON BRIEF

It seems much too early for Easter to be over—all of April stretching ahead of us with Easter already a week old. The relatives, if they came for dinner, have all gone home, and the last egg has been found under the sofa cushion in the living room. So here we are. Waiting. But not quite sure what we're waiting for. Perhaps we are waiting to see if Easter really made any difference to us or to anybody else. We have hung our good suit back in the closet and set the wilted lily out on the back steps. We have closed the door and now, we wait.

It wasn't so different in Jerusalem. Friday and Saturday had passed. Sunday had come, but with the dawn, unexpected, unbelievable news arrived that Jesus had risen from the dead. It was the same word the preacher told us a week ago. But the disciples who gathered in the room had not seen it, so they closed the door and locked it. And they waited. Some, no doubt, wondered if it wasn't time to go home, to get back to whatever they had been doing before all of this happened. To pick up the pieces and start over. But for now, they waited, not quite sure what they were waiting for.

We know the story. Their waiting paid off. Without unlocking the door, Jesus Christ appeared in their midst saying, "Peace be with you." We get little evidence of their reaction, only Jesus' simple greeting as though they should have known he would be there. But a bit later, something rather odd happened. Jesus—who had appeared to Mary Magdalene in the garden and said, "Do not hold on to me"—this same Jesus now invited the disciples to look at his scarred hands and side. Eight days later, Jesus again comes in without knocking and bids Thomas to touch him: "Put your finger here and see my hands. Reach out your hand and put it in my side. Do not doubt but believe" (John 20:27).

Now, this is odd. It's convincing, perhaps, but strange just the same. I come to this part of the story longing to ask questions little children dare to ask before they know better. "If God raised Jesus from the dead, why didn't God fix him up? Why scars? Why the print of nails that you could feel with your fingers?"

We give the child easy answers: "This was how the disciples knew that it was really Jesus" or "This is how we know for certain centuries later." Come now. Mary knew by simply hearing Jesus say her own name out loud. The disciples surely knew when Jesus appeared in their midst without knocking, without the door being opened. "Peace be with you." They didn't ask, "Who are you?" Why wounds in this story?

Who knows? God knows. I cannot be sure of that anymore than I can tell you how God raised Jesus from the sealed tomb. But even the child who dares to ask the question knows there is something in the scars. Something important. Just as it was important for Mary to hear her own name spoken aloud when she was convinced that her name no longer mattered. The scars are not proof, especially for those of us who have not touched them. But the scars remain a witness to the truth.

Why didn't God fix Jesus up? God surely could have. Indeed, at times, it seems that God did! Other Gospel pictures of the resurrected Christ suggest a different kind of body, a body now beyond the limitations and imperfections of earth. "Do not hold on to me," Jesus said to Mary. And in this story, the Resurrected One is not bound by doors or locks, by boundaries of physical space. Yet this is no ghost! Touch my hands, my side. Touch these wounds, and peace be with you.

Can it be that the Gospel word is saying to us in our waiting, "You will not see Jesus Christ unless you see the wounds?" That somehow we must understand that the resurrected Christ is forever the wounded Christ? Living, but never all fixed up. Not bound by death, yet scarred for eternity. Deaf people have a sign for Jesus. Quickly, they make this sign many times during worship: the middle finger of each hand is placed into the palm of the other. Jesus, the one with wounded hands. And when they touch the place, they remember. They hear the name in their own flesh.

We must touch the places where the wounds are. It is not the only place Christ is revealed, but if we deny the wounds, we will see only a glorified Christ whose only name is victory. But the wounded Christ shows us something else: this scarred Jesus does not wait until all fixed up to meet us.

Have you been betrayed by someone you loved? Betrayed by a cause to which you'd given your life? "*Very truly,*" said Jesus, "*one of you will betray me.*"

Have you been let down by your closest friends, by large or small promises set aside without apology? *"Could you not stay awake with me one hour?"*

Have you been afraid to go on living but afraid also to die, uncertain that you have any sense of God's will for your life? *"Father,"* Jesus prayed, *"if it is possible, let this cup pass from me."*

Have you felt utterly alone, abandoned by everyone? *"My God, my God,"* Jesus cried out from the cross, *"why have you forsaken me?"*

Touch the palms of your hands. Jesus was wounded long before the cross, and his wounds touch the wounded places in your life—betrayals and denials, both your own and those made against you. The nails of the manger marked the beginning, for Jesus' birth as a human child marked the beginning of the wounds we all feel as children of the earth. Jesus was not a spiritual baby nor did he float over Galilee without touching the ground. "The Word became flesh" wrote John. Touch the palms of your hands.

Touch the place where the wounds are, in your own life and in the lives of others. You and I have wounds that are almost too painful to bear. Wounds that we cannot talk about even with those we love. We will never be all fixed up, not in this life. The wounded Christ comes to us saying, "Peace be with you." And stop pretending.

A few years ago I saw a play that invited me and others in the audience to end our pretense. Jane Wagner wrote a play called *The Search for Intelligent Life in the Universe;* Lily Tomlin played all the parts, from Trudy the bag lady to Agnes Angst, a punk-rock teenager. Agnes is mad at the world; she dresses to show rebellion against everything. She rails in anger at her father, the biochemist experimenting with new life forms in the laboratory, and at her grandparents in their plastic-covered living room. So Agnes runs away from home—to the House of Pancakes. There, in the trash can, she finds a copy of a book by G. Gordon Liddy of Watergate fame. In the book called *Will* the author has made the claim that human beings have the capacity to do anything they want, to keep pushing on against all odds. He compares this willpower to holding your hand over the flame of a candle: it hurts like hell, but the trick is to learn not to mind. As the first act of the play comes to a close, Agnes is alone on stage. She flings defiance at the whole world, then bends down to light an imaginary candle. One beam of light focuses on her hand as she compares life to the flame of the candle. She echoes Liddy: You hold your hand over its flame and the trick is to learn not to mind. Then all goes dark, and from the darkness Agnes wails "I mind. I mind."

Touch the palms of your hands. The word is Jesus. And the word to us is "I mind." I mind your pain and your loneliness, your abandonment and your despair. Do not pretend that it doesn't matter; do not wait until you're all fixed up. "Put your finger here on the wounds," said Jesus; "put out your hand and place it in my side. Do not be faithless, but believing." My wounded sister, my wounded brother, I mind.

SUGGESTIONS FOR WORSHIP

Call to Worship

LEADER: Come, O Jesus, come to this day; push through the rock that lies in our way[1]

PEOPLE: **That we may walk where the rock is.**

LEADER: Come, O Jesus, come to this day; show us the scars that mark your stay

PEOPLE: **That we may see you where the wounds are.**

LEADER: Come, O Jesus, come to this day; break through our pretense and bid us pray

PEOPLE: **That we may meet you where our wounds are. Amen.**

Prayer of Confession and Assurance of Pardon

O God whose love is stronger than the power of death, hear us and have mercy.

Our failure to believe your word, we confess to you. **O loving God, have mercy.**

Our neglect of the wounded ones in our midst, we confess to you. **O loving God . . .**

Our denial of our own wounds, we confess to you. **O loving God, have mercy.**

Our stubborn self-sufficiency, we confess to you. **O loving God, have mercy.**

Our insistence that truth depends on proof, we confess to you. **O loving God . . .**

(Silence for reflection and attentiveness to our own lives.)

Sisters and brothers, Jesus Christ comes into our midst today saying, "Peace be with you." Peace in your failures and neglect, peace through denial and pride. Peace that is deeper than despair. Live now in the peace of Christ and be at peace with one another. Amen.

Benediction

Touch the palms of your hands. *(congregation joins leader in this sign)*
The Word is Jesus.
Touch the palms of your hands.
The Word speaks peace.
Touch the palms of your hands.
The Word became flesh: Blessed are those who have not seen and yet have come to believe. Amen.

---

1. The idea for the first line of this prayer came from Herb Brokering.

Third Sunday of Easter

Bear Ride Scott

Acts 2:14a, 36-41: The story of the first converts. Peter's Pentecost sermon is responded to by three thousand.

Psalm 116:1-4, 12-19: Thanks is given for deliverance from death. "What shall I return to the LORD?"

I Peter 1:17-23: The congregation is exhorted to live in reverent fear of God, a life of genuine mutual love.

Luke 24:13-35: The risen Christ appears on the road to Emmaus.

REFLECTIONS

When I take off my glasses, I basically can't see. Not often, but sometimes, it's a blessing, for in so doing, I have the dubious privilege of choosing to become entirely oblivious to the world around me. And sometimes that helps. What I have is *presbyopia*. "Presby," of course is from the Greek meaning "old"; "opia," means "vision." Old vision, or old eyes. It is the condition in which one's eyes harden and become inflexible, and thus one is not able to follow the focus as life moves and changes all around. Think on that. Presbyopia, speaking metaphorically, may be a condition of us all, regardless of the state of our eyesight.

The Bible story says that two were going to the village of Emmaus, and they were very busy talking to each other, trying to hash out the events of the week gone by. They were so deep in discussion, in fact, that when Jesus himself came alongside them and even joined in their conversation, sadly, they did not know him. Their sight did not adapt with the requisite flexibility to the new and different focus that faith in the resurrected Christ apparently required. The old had passed away, the new had come, but they could not perceive it. The Gospel says, "but their eyes were kept from recognizing him" (Luke 24:16). The suggestion seems to be that proper optometric adjustments would not have helped. Old eyes.

This story, along with so many others in the Bible and surely stories from our experience, might just lead one to believe that presbyopia is a perceptual condition having less to do with the eyes, and more to do with the receptiveness of our souls. Extending this biblical metaphor even further, do we, with faith, really perceive the gospel message? For surely it is in perceiving the gospel, believing it, trusting Jesus, and subsequently changing our focus accordingly that the challenge of our faith lies.

A SERMON BRIEF

I'm not one of those well-rounded people who studied enough science in college to speak intelligently on the subject in polite company. My lack of scientific understanding has apparently been a source of some embarrassment to my family and friends, for over the past five years, six different people have given me *A Brief History of Time* as a gift—a book by Stephen Hawking, a brilliant physicist, written for the "average layperson." The book, as you probably know, advertises itself as speaking in practical terms about things scientific, things celestial, the beginning of time, the end of time, and how time passes in between.

Well I made it through the first few pages six different times, in fact agreeing enthusiastically with Hawking's citation of Aristotle, who said that the natural state of a body is to be at rest. Perhaps you, like me, experience the truth of that assertion every morning in just trying to get out of bed! Rest is certainly the natural state of my daughter, Cait, and our collie, Sophia (no relation to the goddess), as they both have to be shoved out of bed at dawn.

But Hawking's little book becomes more and more technical and scientific, and each time I utterly surrender by page eleven. But after the sixth and last time, I turned to the jacket flap hoping to uncover the essence of the book. It was on the jacket flap that I read the following startling comment: The brilliant Dr. Hawking "reveals the unsettling possibilities of time running backwards when an expanding universe collapses." *Time running backwards!*

Perhaps one of the reasons I never spent too much time trying to uncover the mysteries of the universe through science was because that was my sister's role in our family system. To this day, whenever any member of the family is faced with a truly puzzling problem in the field of interstellar X-ray astrophysics or quantum mechanics, we just ask Sally.

"And so tell me, " I said to Sally, "tell me about the unsettling possibilities of time running backward when an expanding universe collapses." (Now I understand that I run the risk of assuming that some of you might care. And I also run the risk of deviating irresponsibly from the texts of the day.) But imagine with me for a moment exactly how unsettling it really would be to you and me if, indeed, we might be destined to relive our lives at some vastly future date, backward.

What would you do differently now?

How would you live your life?

How would you change your life?

What different commitments of time and energy would you make?

What questions would you be asking yourself now?

What answers would you be giving yourself now?

How would you talk?

What would you say?

How would you listen?

How would you act?

How would you change?

How would you answer these questions *if* you knew *now* what you'd inevitably know then? These are theological questions of the highest degree, and not altogether inappropriate to the Emmaus text, at that story of clearing the vision and setting priorities along the dusty road of life.

But first of all, according to the family physicist, if I had gotten past page eleven on any of my six opportunities, I would have read that Aristotle was wrong. Friction fooled Aristotle. Einstein made the correction, proving somehow that the natural state of a body was not to be at rest, but that the natural state of a body—a body like yours or like mine for example, or bodies like the two on the road to Emmaus, or even the body of Christ (the Church) we might add—is to be in motion; that is, when something is put into motion, it will stay in motion until someone or something does something to change it. Friction.

(Now I interjected that this is what we might call a "conversion moment" in the church. But the family physicist hates it when I use the laws of physics as theological metaphor.) But ponder and appreciate this with me for a moment: When something is put into motion, it will stay in motion until something or someone does something to stop it. *Friction* is a force that resists the motion.

A conflict.

A collision.

Something that stops you in your tracks and makes you think,

reflect,
pray,
ask questions,
discern,
formulate answers (tentative as they might be),
to decide,
to act,
to act differently,
to rub your metaphorical eyes,
and clear your metaphorical vision.
To Change.

This is like what happened to the travelers when they arrived in Emmaus with their unidentified guest. Surely it was a sort of moment of friction, causing an interruption when that unknown one sat at the table with them, took the bread, blessed and broke it, and gave it to them. The scripture says of this transformational conversion moment that their eyes were opened and they recognized him. And that same hour, it says, they returned to Jerusalem; and they were saying "The Lord has risen indeed" and they told the disciples what happened on the road, and how Jesus had been made known to them in the breaking of the bread. And because of that moment—the recognition, the turn about, the change in mind and action—the saving gospel news was out, and the world was changed.

We are given moments like this in our lives, when the substance of the gospel collides with the substance of the world and of our lives. Friction, as it were, happens, and we are called out
to feel,
to think,
to pray,
to question,
to answer,
to choose,
to respond,
to change.

It is a conversion moment. We are always being given conversion moments. And choosing at those moments who we are to be and what we are to be about defines us and defines the faith unalterably and forever—world with or without end, Einstein and Hawking notwithstanding.

Friction fooled Aristotle; let it not fool us. In a recent edition of *News of the Weird*, it was reported that a thirty-two-year-old woman who worked in the wardrobe department of Universal Studios in Hollywood got lost while driving on the lot and found herself following a tram. The tram, carrying tourists, proceeded down the middle of the "Red Sea" attraction, in which the waters are mechanically "parted" for the tram. However, at the instant the tram completes the trip, the water is released, and the woman was thus trapped in the middle of the "sea" for an hour until firefighters rescued her. Sometimes it feels like we're trapped in the middle of the Red Sea.

Friction fooled Aristotle; let it not fool us. More serious moments of friction, like urban challenges, outrageous ballot measures, and politicians of less than sparkling credentials; conflicts and controversies within the church; and challenges to community and conscience form faith and faithful action. And when we are faithful, our eyes are opened, as it were, and we are changed. "Were not our hearts burning within us while he was talking to us on the road?" they asked of their chance encounter with the risen Jesus. Do not our hearts burn within us when we have our God-given chance meetings with Jesus as well?

In his unpublished manuscript, which exquisitely defines the state of the Presbyterian Church in our day, my friend and colleague Jack Rogers makes the following helpful observation about community and change: "Experience is important. It colors our community worldview. It influences the way we read Scripture, how we listen to others, and the way we make decisions." But, he adds that's not where our unity lies. Our unity lies in something external to us; specifically, our unity lies in Christ.

"Experience" he continues, "is the principle of change. It keeps our unity from being uniformity. . . . The principles of continuity must be outside ourselves to which we all have common reference." Jesus meets us on the road through Scripture and sacraments and we perceive him (to the extent we are able and receptive) and we are changed. Do not our hearts burn within us when we are on that road with him?

The family physicist admits that scientists can tell us what happened at one billionth of a second after the world was formed, and even earlier, if you are curious enough to want to know. They can tell you about the near beginning of time, how time travels from one end to the other (and apparently, possibly, back again!), and why time travels at different rates in different contexts (unscientifically, we know them as good days and bad days), and they can tell us what might happen when time is no more. But it is up to us to decide what to do with the time we are given—what to do and make of our own time.

SUGGESTIONS FOR WORSHIP

Call to Worship (Psalm 116 adapted)

LEADER: What shall we return to God for the bounty with which God has filled our lives?

PEOPLE: We will lift up the cup of salvation and call on God's name.

LEADER: We will pay our vows to the Lord in the presence of all the people.

PEOPLE: O Lord, you have heard our voice, you inclined your ear to us,

ALL: And we will call upon you as long as we live.

Prayer of Confession

Gracious God, we who lift your cup and eat your bread confess that we often do so unthinkingly, unfeelingly. We do not expect to see you. We do not expect you to hear us. Ultimately, we really believe everything depends on us. Forgive us, we pray. Kindle in us an ability to walk humbly and listen closely to your presence in our midst. In your name, we pray. Amen.

Assurance of Pardon (Acts 2 adapted)

For the promise is to you and to your children and to all who are far away.
Everyone whom the Lord our God calls,
Believe the Good News.
In Jesus Christ, we are forgiven!

Benediction (I Pet. 1:22)

Now that you have purified your souls by your obedience to the truth so that you have genuine mutual love, love one another deeply from the heart.

Fifth Sunday of Easter

Edwina Hunter

Acts 7:55-60: The stoning of Stephen. At the end of his speech before the council, Stephen has a vision of Jesus standing at the right hand of God. The listeners are enraged and drag him outside of the city to stone him.

Psalm 31:1-5, 15-16: A prayer for deliverance from enemies. "My times are in your hand."

I Peter 2:2-10: The living stone is rejected by mortals but chosen by God. So, too, are the letter's recipients chosen—chosen to proclaim God's mighty acts.

John 14:1-14: "Do not let your hearts be troubled." Jesus is the way to God and is going to prepare a place for his disciples. Then "the one who believes in me will also do the works that I do."

REFLECTIONS

All my life I have felt drawn to Stephen. As a little girl in Sunday school, I liked Stephen. Later as a teenager, I saw him as a biblical hero. And for some reason, now that I have gray hair, and have lived my own journey of faith for more than fifty years, Stephen is more real to me than ever.

This really is odd, you know. Stephen is mentioned in chapters six and seven and the second verse of chapter eight in Acts and nowhere else in the Bible. Maybe that's why many others have been drawn to Stephen imaginatively, too. We have known so few facts about him that we can fill in all the details ourselves.

For example, when I was a little girl, Stephen was kind of a New Testament David figure to me. The young David. The one who was out in the fields with his sheep and his harp, and suddenly was called in and anointed with oil, and told he was to be king of Israel. The young David who had such a sense of his own immortality and strength that he thought he could do anything. For me, the young Stephen I visualized was a great deal like that. But let's look at his story—at how his name first appears.

A SERMON BRIEF

You remember what it says early in Acts 6: "The disciples were increasing in number." There must have been thousands and thousands by then. There were three thousand after Peter preached and many others were added every day. Anyway, the Hellenists who had become believers "murmured against" the Hebrew believers because the widows of the Hellenists were being neglected in the daily distribution. Now, "murmured against" is a great biblical phrase for saying the Hellenists were gossiping and complaining and stirring up a bit of trouble. Well, Peter and John and the other apostles heard the complaints and decided it was time to respond. So they told the people that since they—the apostles—were so busy preaching (isn't that just the way!), the people should select seven others—people of good reputation, full of the Spirit and wisdom—whom the apostles could appoint to the job of waiting tables! Did you ever read such qualifications listed in the want-ad section of your paper? "Waiter wanted: Only those persons should apply who have a good reputation and are filled with Spirit and wisdom."

Stephen and six others were chosen—and set aside—to wait tables! It is said of Stephen that he was not only full of the Spirit and wisdom, he was also full of faith. Maybe that is a dangerous combination.

At any rate, we never read anything about Stephen waiting tables! Why, we expect people to do the jobs for which they are hired and appointed. They aren't supposed to go off doing other people's jobs. Maybe it was this side of Stephen that appealed to my child self. He didn't stay where he was told to. He did the unexpected. He did what God called him to do. Maybe the apostles had to wind up waiting on tables after all! Not just preaching, but waiting on tables too! Because Stephen did great signs and wonders among the people. Now that's what Acts says Stephen did. We don't know exactly what that means. Luke never tells us. So we can use our imaginations again. And as a child that's just what I did.

As a child I could see young Stephen—he was always young when I was a child—striding through the streets. Children were at play in the streets and one suddenly ran out in the very path of a charging Roman chariot. She would be killed! But no, Stephen was there, and somehow, in his youth and quickness and strength, he ran in front of the chariot, picked the child up in his arms and swept them both to safety. In my child's mind, signs and wonders were the kinds of things done by a handsome idealistic youth. As a teenager and all through my young adult years, I could see Stephen as a young man—still handsome and still idealistic, by all means. Surely, it was idealism about how people ought to be, how the world should respond to Christ and the crucifixion of Christ that drove Stephen to take all sorts of risks, that drove him to get into the trouble he did with the authorities, that drove him to follow the way of Christ to the extent that his story became a parallel of the Christ story. Because Stephen did what he believed God wanted him to do, people began spreading false stories about him, telling lies about him, just as they had against Jesus. They set him up. They found false witnesses who were willing to tell lies in public. And the bishop, or the high priest, or the executive minister came and asked him, "Are these things so?"

Then this courageous young man began to preach. He did not answer the question he had been asked, he began to preach as God led him to do. He had been appointed to wait tables but God had called him to preach! And preach he did. He began with God's call to Abraham and traced the history of God's workings with God's people from that time forward. When he got to the story of Moses at the burning bush, he became truly eloquent. I could see Stephen standing there, tall and strong, having awed his high-ranking accusers into silence. I could see him standing, head thrown back, voice resonant and strong, eyes flashing, as he told them about Moses and his call. About how Moses saw a bush burning that would not be consumed. About how God spoke to Moses out of that bush and told him he was standing on holy ground.

Oh, Stephen, at that very moment I feared for you. Somehow I knew that you, too, had seen your burning bush and you, too, had answered the call of God, and Stephen, you, too, wouldn't stop until you had spoken what God wanted you to say.

And Stephen didn't stop. He went on preaching until he had said what God wanted him to stay. And I stand here before you this morning in my gray-haired years and I still see Stephen. But I no longer see him as the tall, handsome young man with flashing eyes. Now, I see him at about my age, I guess. Still straight, perhaps not quite as tall, his face wearing lines of suffering and character and inner strength, his eyes the eyes of one who has seen the heights and depths of human experience and still loves.

And I see determination and full knowledge of the consequences of his actions. Drawing himself together he looks at his accusers directly and addresses them in words of such damning indictment that, for those moments, they know themselves to be the accused and he the accuser. He says "You stiff-necked people, uncircumcised in heart and ears, you are forever opposing the Holy Spirit, just as your ancestors used to do. Which of the prophets did your ancestors not persecute? They killed those who foretold the coming of the Righteous One, and now you have become his betrayers and murderers. You are the ones that received the law as ordained by angels, and yet you have not kept it" (Acts 7:51-53).

Oh, Stephen, you were indeed one who followed the way. Did you have to do it so literally? So very much like Jesus? Peter preached and accused those who listened to him, and thousands repented and became believers. You preached and they stoned you to death. What was the difference? Was it because Peter had others standing with him that he was heard differently? Were you left out there all by yourself? Left alone, no one standing with you? Like Jesus?

Stephen, in the very midst of the stones pounding against you, how were you able to pray as you did? Why, you prayed for God to forgive those who were stoning you even as Jesus prayed for God to forgive those who crucified him. Stephen, you were a man filled with the Spirit and with faith. Because you spoke as you did and died as you did, and because you prayed as you did, Saul became Paul and Paul took the Good News of Jesus Christ to the Gentiles; and because Paul did this, here we sit this morning. Stephen, we are your descendants. Oh, that we would act like it! Oh, that we, too, would be, in truth, followers of the way. Oh, that we too, would live and speak what God wants us to live and speak even if it means we are stoned—literally or verbally. But please, God, let there be those who come to stand with us. Please. We don't want to stand alone.

One more thing. As a teacher I have to remind you: There are Stephens and Stephanies who have grown up, who are growing up in our churches, who know that God is calling them, some to wait tables, all to preach the gospel in his or her own way. God is not calling just the Stephanies to wait tables! God is also calling Stephens to wait tables and Stephanies to preach!

Please, as a church, as the people of this church, make a personal and financial commitment to stand with those Stephens and Stephanies who have been rallied up by God. Some are young and idealistic; some are a bit older and some are as gray-haired as I. They can all be so easily stoned to death, or simply ignored, or given little or no opportunity to preach, unless the people of God stand with them as the eleven stood with Peter.

Suggestions for Worship

Call to Worship (Ps. 31:3, 15-16 adapted)

LEADER: The Lord is our rock and our fortress.

PEOPLE: A shelter in the time of storm.

LEADER: Our times are in your hand, O God.

PEOPLE: Deliver us from the hands of our enemies.

LEADER: Let your face shine upon us, O God.

ALL: And save us in your steadfast love.

Prayer of Confession

We are not so different from those who put Stephen on trial, O God. We have been stiff-necked. We have resisted the Holy Spirit. We have ignored prophets and been enraged by truth-tellers. We have received the word of God and not kept it. Forgive us, O God of mercy. Turn us and heal us so that we may stand with you and for you. In the name of Jesus Christ, we pray. Amen.

Assurance of Pardon (I Pet. 2:9-10 adapted)

Now you are God's own people, called out of the darkness and into the light. Once you were no people, but now you are God's people; once you had not received mercy, but now you have received mercy. Friends, believe the good news. In Jesus Christ, we are forgiven.

Charge and Benediction

Jesus says that those who believe in him will also do the works he does, and greater works than these, even. Go out in boldness then, knowing that Christ has promised to do whatever you ask in his name. And may the grace of Christ sustain you, the love of God surround you, and the Holy Spirit strengthen you now and forevermore.

Sixth Sunday of Easter

Edwina Hunter

Acts 17:22-31: Paul's speech at the Areopagus. Distressed to find the city full of idols, Paul argues with the Athenians that their unknown god is really THE God—the one who raised Jesus from the dead.

Psalm 66:8-20: God's goodness is praised. "Bless our God . . . who has kept us among the living, and has not let our feet slip."

I Peter 3:13-17: Suffering for doing good is better than suffering for doing evil. "Always be ready to make your defense to anyone who demands from you an accounting for the hope that is in you."

John 14:15-21, 23: Jesus promised to send the Holy Spirit, who will abide with and in the disciples.

REFLECTIONS

"If you love me. . . ." I wonder how many times those words have been said by a wife to a husband, by a husband to a wife, by a girlfriend to a boyfriend, by a child to a parent, by a parent to a child? But, have you noticed, usually it's put in the past tense: "If you loved me, you would. . . ." The sentence can be finished with any number of things. You would take out the trash when you said you would. You would buy me that dress or coat or ring you know I want. You would have my dinner ready when I get home from work. You would agree to have my parents come live with us. You would buy me an ice-cream cone! "If you loved me, you would. . . ."

Or sometimes it's said, "If you loved me you wouldn't. . . . If you loved me you wouldn't nag me all the time. If you loved me, you wouldn't leave me alone so much of the time. If you loved me you wouldn't make me eat this spinach. If you loved me, you wouldn't keep drinking . . . or smoking." "If you loved me. . . ."

Have you ever said it to anyone? I certainly have. If you loved me you would do exactly what I want you to do. If you loved me you would never do what I do not want you to do. When we say it, we are usually trying to get the other person to do something because that something will benefit us. Even if we say it about something as serious as drinking too much, usually our motivation is less than clear. We don't want to have to contend with the problem. We don't want to be embarrassed by the behavior. Only at our best moments is it because we are genuinely concerned for the well-being of the other person. Only at our best moments are we feeling our deep love for the other person when we say, "If you loved me. . . ."

When Jesus said, "If you love me . . ." how different it was. Jesus said, "If you love me" and then he said, "you will keep my commandments." But that doesn't sound very different, you say. He, too, wanted something—he wanted his commandments to be kept. But what *were* his commandments? Earlier in John 13, he said it very clearly: "I give you a new commandment, that you love one another. Just as I have loved you, you also should love one another. By this everyone will know that you are my disciples, if you have love for one another" (John 13:34-35).

And now he says, "If you love me, you will keep my commandments. And I will pray to God and God will give you another Counselor, to be with you forever, even the Spirit of truth whom the world cannot receive, because it neither sees the Spirit nor knows the Spirit; you know the Spirit, for the Spirit dwells with (is at home) with you, and will be with you." The natural result of our loving as Christ loves is that the Spirit will dwell with us—will be *at home* within us.

A Sermon Brief

Over the years, I have participated in many weddings but I don't remember any wedding so joyful as the one this past Friday night. I was asked to give the homily and to otherwise assist in the ceremony for two of the students with whom I went to the Philippines. Lynn Rhodes, the faculty member who arranged the trip, officiated. But Phil and Grace themselves wrote and spoke their marriage vows as they exchanged their rings. The wedding was at Pacific School of Religion. Their families had come long distances to be there, but understood their need to be married in the community of which they have been so much a part. I think every student on campus as well as many from off campus was present. The room was packed.

Phil and Grace are so deeply loved by the entire community. Even as I remember, I feel this glow inside me at the marvelous spontaneity of response. They had asked Lynn for an informal declaration of marriage after their vows and exchange of rings. So she said a few words and then said, with a smile in her voice and on her face, "And so you are married!" The whole place erupted in applause and cheers that went on and on. I began to expect everyone to give them a standing ovation.

Their families had stood with us for the exchange of the rings and vows. And after the prayer of blessing that I prayed, the family members welcomed their new son or daughter into their families with hugs, the gift of a flower, and whispered words. Then I told the gathered congregation that I would ask them three questions and they could respond in any way they chose. The three questions were: "Do you celebrate with Phil and Grace the choice they have made to marry? Will you do all in your power to support and care for them in this marriage? Will you challenge and support them to be faithful to God's call for justice in our world?"

I wish you could have heard the response. The congregation seemingly cheered as they voiced an enthusiastic "Yes!" to each question and then, again, there was sustained applause and affirmation. You see, these are two rather quiet people. But their commitment to justice, their commitment to doing the work of Christ is profound and has been an uncommon witness on that campus. The summer after our January trip to the Philippines they returned to Manila to do clinical pastoral education in a hospital there. That was the summer after Corazon Aquino's election. It was a very hard time for them as they ministered to people in the hospital, to people who were very ill with malnutrition, to people who were dying of starvation, and to parents of babies who were dying because they never really had a chance.

The reason that wedding Friday was such a joy-filled occasion was because Grace and Phil have already given and are continuing to give a lived-out answer to Christ. Christ said to them, "If you love me, you will keep my commandments. . . . If you love me, you will love my children and serve my children wherever they are in need." The reason that wedding Friday was such a joy-filled occasion is that Phil and Grace had written their vows so they could say to each other, "If you love me, together we will love others and seek justice for those who do not have justice. If you love me, you will continue to grow in Christ and you will help me grow in Christ. If you love me, you will be for me a home, a haven, where I can come to be renewed and healed, where we can heal each other, so we can return to the work Christ calls us to do."

Oh, I know Grace and Phil are young and idealistic and marriages often start out with joy that's lost in the everydayness of life. Please God, that won't be so for them. And I can't help believing their marriage has a better chance than most because from the very beginning, their "If you love me's . . ." are responses to the "If you love me, you will keep my commandments," of Christ.

I can't imagine that their lives will be easy. That isn't what it means to follow the Way. To keep the commandments of Jesus and love one another is about the hardest thing anybody ever tried to do. Sometimes that kind of love—loving others as Jesus loved us—gets us into trouble. If it doesn't, then we can be sure we aren't loving others as Jesus loved us. Look at the trouble Jesus got into because he loved us. That kind of love is not sentimental and pretty all the time. It is tough and hard and active. It is a radical love. It steps on the toes of those who want things done a certain way all the time.

What we often forget is that in loving us and all sorts of strange and outcast people, Jesus violated the rules. He angered those in authority. He angered those religious leaders who thought things had to be done a certain way. And he paid the price.

Let's see if we can understand this. Put in our way of looking at things, a similar thing would be if we decided as a congregation that we were going to support something that our regional or national church leaders are against. What if we came to believe deeply that the way we are to show our love for Christ was to support something that many of our church leaders and even most other churches are against? Let me give you a specific example. I had a young man in my class this semester who had been doing his field education at Delores Street Baptist Church in San Francisco. I don't know what you know about that church, but it is located in an area of the city where there is a large gay population. The church has been Southern Baptist, but because the congregations include persons who are gay and people with AIDS, the church is no longer wanted by the Southern Baptists. Church members have begun to pursue the possibility of affiliating with American Baptists but they have been led to understand they might not be so welcome with us either. Believe me, if our congregation spent time in prayer and in seeking the mind of Christ and, through that, came to believe that advocacy for Delores Street Baptist Church to become American Baptist would be a way of fulfilling Christ's command to love one another, we would be immediately suspect. We, as Christ, would be hobnobbing with the outcast, sitting down to dinner with sinners. In the eyes of many, that is exactly what we would be doing.

Even if we said, "We do this because Christ told us to love one another and because we believe Christ is leading us to do this," we would pay a price.

That is the kind of thing for which Jesus tried to prepare his disciples—for paying the price, for suffering because they had taken a stand for Christ, for being persecuted because they had tried to follow his command to love across all lines. Sometimes we do something foolish and wrong and bring something on ourselves and we try to say we are suffering for Christ's sake. Oh, I firmly believe God can bring good out of anything—even out of the worst things we do in our lives. But suffering for Christ's sake means that we choose to love as Christ loves, not in order to be a martyr, but because that's simply the way we must walk, and suffering or misunderstanding or outright persecution comes as a result. As I said before, loving the way Christ wants us to love is radical and it is rarely understood or commended. Even by other Christians.

In this context, perhaps we can hear our I Peter passage a little better: "But even if you do suffer for doing what is right, you are blessed. Do not fear what they fear, and do not be intimidated, but in your hearts sanctify Christ as Lord. Always be ready to make your defense to anyone who demands from you an accounting for the hope that is in you; yet do it with gentleness and reverence. Keep your conscience clear, so that, when you are maligned, those who abuse you for your good conduct in Christ may be put to shame. For it is better to suffer for doing good, if suffering should be God's will, than to suffer for doing evil" (vv. 14-17).

Jesus tells us today, " 'If you love me . . . keep my commandments. If you love me, love one another.' If you love me, try loving the outcast, the ones others don't love. Try loving them as I loved the woman at the well, the woman taken in adultery, the tax collector, the publican, the leper. 'If you love me . . .' and act on that love, you may have to pay the price. I did, for loving you." Amen.

SUGGESTIONS FOR WORSHIP

Call to Worship (Ps. 66:8-9, 16 adapted)

LEADER: Blessed be our God, O peoples,

PEOPLE: Let the sound of God's praise be heard,

LEADER: Who has kept us among the living

PEOPLE: And has not let our feet slip.

LEADER: Come and hear, all you that fear God,

PEOPLE: And I will tell what God has done for me.

LEADER: Blessed be our God, O peoples,

ALL: **Let the sound of God's praise be heard.**

Prayer of the People

God of grace and glory, we come before you like a child surprised to find another Easter egg hidden at the bottom of the basket.[1] We are bedazzled by the beauty with which you have planted our lives. These days, this beauty seems to pop and plop and perk all around us. Our eyes are swimming, our ears are humming, and we are grateful. We are grateful that you are not a stingy God holding back the color and the sap and the melody. You are a God who lays on the purple with a heavy hand, who is extravagant with soft breezes and lavish with trumpet fanfares, who doesn't mind sharing it all with us. You overwhelm us. How can we thank you for the beauty of our days and the ease of our nights?

We think of those whose days are difficult and whose nights are uneasy and we ask you to expand and amplify our efforts to alleviate suffering, comfort the grieving, and guide the doubtful. We give you thanks that you are not only a God of loveliness—of sunbeams and tulips—but a God of power and might who is on the side of the needy. Strengthen us in your love, that we might walk with you and keep your commandments. In the name of Jesus Christ, we pray. Amen.

Benediction (John 14:18, 20)

Jesus said, "I will not leave you orphaned; I am coming to you. . . . On that day you will know that I am in God and you in me and I in you."

---

1. The first line of this prayer is taken from Robert Raines, "Let Me Be Like a Child, Surprised" in *Lord Could You Make It a Little Better?* (Waco: Word, 1972), p. 85.

Ascension Day

Anne Miner-Pearson

Acts 1:1-11: Jesus is taken up into heaven while the disciples stand watching.

Psalm 47: "Clap your hands, all you peoples. . . . God has gone up with a shout."

Ephesians 1:15-23: Paul prays that the Ephesians may know the greatness of God's power that raised Christ from the dead, seated him in heavenly places, and put all things under his feet.

Luke 24:44-53: The Gospel ends with Jesus opening the disciples minds to understand the scriptures and being "carried up into heaven."

REFLECTIONS

Leave-taking is a frequent experience in every aspect of our personal and corporate life. Few of us still live in the town in which we grew up. No longer do most of us work for the same company or in the same location until retirement. With the increased divorce rate, young children leave one life context and struggle to navigate between two new ones. Even saying good-bye to this earthly life is in the news as we debate the merits and legality of euthanasia. Can we choose the way and time of our final farewell? As a nation, we are aware of the loss of community, institutional trust, and moral underpinnings. In significant ways, we have left life as we have known it, often without an opportunity to understand the dynamics or deal with the emotions.

The members of my suburban congregation in St. Paul, Minnesota, have experienced leave-taking. Divorce has changed many family units. Company buyouts and downsizing have affected others. Few still live close to the neighborhood where they had played ball or walked to school as children. Some in the parish have struggled with the medical and spiritual issues as a parent aged and died. With varied degrees of success and peace, all had dealt with having to say good-bye. Some good-byes were chosen. Others were thrust upon them. All knew about leaving.

On this Sunday after Ascension, another leaving is taking place. I have accepted a call as rector of an Episcopal congregation in San Diego. For me, twenty years of living in Minnesota are coming to a close. For this congregation, my time as their first rector is ending after ten years. Leaving a community and losing a leader are not easy times. The head can decipher the logic, but the heart is left with feelings of emptiness and fear. Uncertainty closes in like an unwelcome predator. Anger is a possibility. More is unknown than known. The urges to control and move rapidly through this time are strong ones. A sense of grief and anxiety is in the air mixed with strands of excitement and celebration.

A SERMON BRIEF

During a group reflection on the passage in the Acts of the Apostle, I was teasingly accused of tampering with the assigned readings for this Sunday. Just too much coincidence, someone thought, to have passages about Jesus leaving at this time of my leaving. However, I'm innocent except for my slipping the Ascension readings from Thursday to Sunday. But the connections didn't pass unnoticed.

There's a lot of leaving going on in these readings. The Acts and the Gospel passages are accounts of Jesus' final physical departure from the disciples. In dramatic detail, we catch the scene. Forty days after the Resurrection, he walks with them as far as Bethany. He reminds them of God's promised power. They are to wait in Jerusalem. They are to be witnesses to the new life they have experienced from Jesus' life, death, and resurrection. Then, a blessing, a cloud. Jesus is gone.

I wonder what goes on in the disciples' heads. Or more important, in their hearts. Even after all they have been through—the crucifixion, the resurrection, the numerous encounters with Jesus—are they prepared for Jesus' leaving? Are they ready for their leader to be gone and to be "on their own"? Do they think they have what it takes to continue to be disciples, to be those "witnesses" Jesus is asking them to be?

Are any of us ever really ready for "leaving"? Are we ever prepared to have a significant person depart? Do we ever think that we can "make it on our own" and find the resources within and among us to not just simply "carry on," but to be all that we are called to be? No, and I suspect that the disciples are no more ready or prepared for leaving than any of us—whether the leaving is my departure from St. Anne's; one's children from home for college, marriage, or jobs; someone we love leaving her home to live in a resident care facility; or a loved one from this life to eternal life with God.

Leaving is powerful. Leaving is complex. The Gospel story tells of the disciples returning to the Temple in Jerusalem praising and rejoicing. Acts tells another version: The disciples just stand there and look at the place where they last see Jesus. Leaving is joy and absence. There is a power in leaving.

Leaving creates a time for learning more about trust, about faith in God. Jesus works all of his ministry to point both disciples and enemies beyond him to God. The message of Jesus is fundamentally an invitation to enter into a conscious and constant relationship with God. That's a hard message to get. The disciples have it confused and want to hang on to Jesus. We have trouble and want to hang on to people who are only companions on the journey. As important as we are for one another, we are not saved or made whole solely by being with one another. Clergy don't sustain Christians and congregations. God does.

Part of the power of leaving St. Anne's is our relearning the message of Jesus' ascension. All Souls' Episcopal Church in San Diego had the chance to relearn the message over the last two years without a rector. When I arrive at my new church, all of us will have to work not to forget the power of that learning and think that "the savior has arrived"! It's so tempting. You will be tempted when you call your next rector, but the point is not physical bodies—not even Jesus' physical body. The point is trusting in *God,* believing in God's promise to be present and gracious with the gifts of the Holy Spirit.

We can grow to trust God in the leaving. That's part of the power of leaving. For leaving faces us with hearing hard answers and answering hard questions. Leaving is not merely emptiness. We can walk around the space and wonder. We can examine our assumptions. Is it really true that people abandon one another when someone else is gone? Does fear truly have more power than commitment and hope?

We test the limits of knowing. Like the disciples, we ask, "Lord, is this the time when . . . ?" We want all uncertainties erased. We want clarity and road maps and time lines. Then we learn another part of the power of leaving: hearing hard answers. "It is not for you to know." Leaving confronts us with the reality that there are some things beyond our knowing—maybe for just a time, maybe forever. For us as bright, successful, educated Americans, that's difficult. "It is not for you to know." Some things are not knowable . . . yet.

Like what the interim time will bring or what ministry Daniel, my husband, will be called to in California. Other things are simply not our business. As someone told me on a Teens Encounter Christ weekend, "That's not in a pile of life." Pieces of life belong to other people and to God. Leaving is a reminder of that. That's part of the power of leaving.

Yet, hearing hard answers is not all there is to it. When we are in a time of leaving, we also answer hard questions. Two men dressed in white robes stand by the disciples and ask, "Why do you stand looking up toward heaven?" (Acts 1:11). We can't help asking "why?" Leaving challenges us to probe our understanding of ourselves and the situation. Of course, we need to gather all the facts. We try to be logical and rational. But, at some point, we arrive at the "why?" "Why" goes beyond the facts and beyond what our reasoning can tell us. "Why" unlocks our story. "Why" is the world of imagination and intuition. "Why" opens us to see connections, to speculate on possibilities. Sure, "why" can lead to blaming and judging, but not necessarily. In a time of leaving, "why" can lead us to honestly discover who we are *now* and give us the courage to live into that self. There is a power in leaving.

Yet, the power of leaving doesn't come all at once, thankfully. That might be overwhelming. God is more gentle with us than that. A time of leaving is a time of waiting. The disciples are told to wait in Jerusalem. There is more to come. There is more than can be seen or known at this time. Waiting. Waiting.

Waiting is no easier for us than not knowing. Our schools and cultures have formed us well. Immediacy and intelligence are important to us. Few of us like delay or admitting that we don't know something. Those are probably two key reasons why leaving is so difficult. Leaving delays the expected flow of life. We are left with unknowns. We must wait and watch. Jesus' ascension is about waiting and watching for gifts. A prayer in Ephesians names these gifts: a spirit of wisdom and revelation, hope, and enlighted eyes of the heart (see vv. 17-18). Waiting witnesses to belief in prayer and the gifts.

There is power in leaving, power in learning to trust in God more and more, to hear hard answers, to answer hard questions, and to wait for the promise and gifts to come. There is power in leaving because of what Jesus left to us. Jesus left us his power, a power "God put . . . to work . . . when he raised him from the dead and seated him at his right hand in the heavenly places . . ." (Eph. 1:20). God's power transforms Jesus and Jesus' leaving transfers that power to us. Jesus' power is to teach, heal, forgive, and gather into communion with Jesus' new body: the church. God's power witnessed by Jesus in his life, death, and resurrection is now in a body that lives beyond Jesus of Nazareth. Indeed, God's power lives in St. Anne's and All Souls', in all Christian denominations, and yes, I believe, in all holy men and women who gather to praise and rejoice in God. That's the power of Jesus' leaving. That's the power Jesus leaves us in our leaving.

SUGGESTIONS FOR WORSHIP

Call to Worship (Psalm 47 adapted)

LEADER: Clap your hands, all you peoples.

PEOPLE: Shout to God with songs of joy.

LEADER: God has gone up with a shout.

PEOPLE: Sing praises to God who rules over all the earth.

LEADER: Sing praises to God, sing praises.

ALL: Let all the people gather to praise the Lord.

Prayer of Confession

Gracious God, you left us with a charge to carry your word to the ends of the earth, but we are weary. You left us with a challenge to open ourselves to the Holy Spirit, but we are cautious. You left us gazing upward and standing idly by; some of us are there still. Forgive us, O God, and fill us with power from above. In the name of Jesus Christ we pray. Amen.

Assurance of Pardon

LEADER: As far as the east is from the west, so far has God removed our sins from us. Friends, believe the Good News.

PEOPLE: In Jesus Christ we are forgiven.

ALL: Alleluia! Amen.

Benediction (Acts 1:8)

"But you will receive power when the Holy Spirit has come upon you; and you will be my witnesses . . . to the ends of the earth."

Seventh Sunday of Easter

Edwina Hunter

Acts 1:6-14: The story of Jesus' ascension includes a promise that the disciples will receive power when the Holy Spirit comes upon them.

Psalm 68:1-10: Scholars sometimes refer to this psalm as the most difficult to interpret. The selected verses praise God's protectiveness and faithfulness.

I Peter 4:12-14: Inasmuch as we share Christ's suffering we also share his glory.

I Peter 5:6-11: The letter concludes with several exhortations and a benediction.

John 17:1-11: Jesus' high-priestly prayer.

REFLECTIONS

"That they may be one." What exactly do those words mean? Certainly they are a part of Jesus' prayer in John 17:11. But what do they mean? Today is celebrated in many churches as Ascension Sunday. The Acts reading this morning is the story of the ascension of Jesus and the promise he gave the disciples that they would receive power in the coming of the Holy Spirit and then they would become witnesses in Jerusalem, Samaria, and throughout the world. The disciples received this promise, saw him taken out of their sight, and then returned together to Jerusalem to the upper room and waited and prayed. Of course when we say "disciples" we do not mean simply the apostles, but all the men and women and probably children who followed Jesus. They were all disciples, followers, students, friends of Jesus.

Many biblical scholars believe that the prayer Jesus prayed in John 17 is a prayer of the risen Christ prayed within the hearing of the disciples. Seen this way, it is possible to link Jesus' prayer with the prayers the disciples prayed in the upper room.

As I tried to understand this prayer of Jesus and its implications for the disciples and us, I found that what I wanted to do was ask Peter, "You heard Jesus pray that way. What did that prayer mean to you?" I wanted to do that and so, in my imagination, I did. And you know, I think I heard him answer.

A SERMON BRIEF

"Believe me. When Jesus prays for you, something happens. I had no idea what it would mean to me—to all of us—when he prayed as he did. You see, it was after the Resurrection and we had finally come to understand that he would be leaving us to be with God. We felt such a need for his presence. We had been a weak bunch all along. Perhaps I should speak for myself. I was so weak that I denied him. I denied Jesus, the One whom I love above all else. That should give you some idea about how weak I was.

"Anyway, it seemed strange to us that the risen Christ should still feel the need to pray. He had just told us he was going to be with God. Then he told us that we would be scattered but we were to be of good cheer. Good cheer? Happy? Now I ask you, Did that make sense? Another riddle! But then he began to pray. First he prayed for himself. I had never heard him pray for himself in quite that way. He was asking God to glorify him and reminding God about how he had taught us. I was listening and wondering about that so hard when, suddenly, I realized he was praying for us! He said God had given us to him and we belonged to God. He told God he wasn't in the world anymore but we were. And just in the way he said it, I knew he was concerned about us. Then he prayed, and I'll never forget these words. 'Protect them in your name that you have given me, so that they may be one, as we are one' (John 17:11).

"Well, you asked me what those words meant to me. I confess, I didn't understand, but I wanted to. I mean, I not only wanted to understand, I wanted to do what he said. I wanted to be one with Jesus, with God, with all the other disciples. I needed us all to be part of one another. I was afraid everything was going to be just too hard if we weren't. But I had no idea at all what it would mean if that prayer was answered. And it was. It really was.

"Let me just give you an example about how it worked. You see, right after Jesus was taken up out of our sight, we all did as he told us and went back to Jerusalem together to pray and wait. He had told us the Holy Spirit would come and give us power. We weren't too sure what that meant either. But we waited and prayed. And sure enough, something happened! I mean the Holy Spirit happened! And I could tell you a lot about that, but right now just let me tell you that we began to suspect that this was a part of the answer to Jesus' prayer. We did feel more oneness now than we had ever felt before. We were together in a way we had never been before. And things happened because of that.

"Why one day John and I were on our way to the temple to pray. And there by the temple gate was a man who was lame. He was begging for alms and we didn't have any money. But almost before I knew what I was doing I was offering him healing! Somehow I knew I was one with him! That what affected him affected me. I had to reach out to him. That's when I knew I was one with Jesus, too. It was his power in John and me that healed that man.

"Well, that was one time, but probably what I remember best is an experience that started out with a dream—actually, it was more like a nightmare. I was up on the roof asleep and I had this dream—not once, but three times! I dreamed that a great sheet came down from heaven and in it were the most terrible unclean things—all kinds of animals and snakes and birds. And I heard a voice telling me to get up and kill those things and eat them. But I knew better. I had never eaten anything unclean and I wasn't about to begin. Sure, I was hungry but not that hungry. Well, as I said it happened three times. And I heard that same voice, which I knew to be the voice of the risen Christ, telling me, 'What God has made clean, you must not call profane' (Acts 10:15). Well, after the third time, the thing was taken back up and I fully awoke, and then there I was trying to figure it out. It wasn't unlike some of the riddles Jesus had left us with!

"A little while later I found out what it was all about. A messenger came and wanted me to go to the home of a man named Cornelius—a Gentile! Then I heard the Spirit telling me to go immediately to that house! Well, you would have to know just how I felt about Gentiles to know how hard that was for me. It was even worse than eating unclean food! But I went. And by now you must know what happened. I preached and those Gentiles believed! Why, the Holy Spirit fell on them just as the Spirit had fallen on us! What was I to do? Here was further proof that Jesus' prayer was answered. We were one—not only with one another—but with Gentiles! And they were one with us and with God.

"That was a real revelation. One that changed the course of history. Why, all of you wouldn't be sitting here today worshiping the Christ if all of us back there hadn't become convinced that we were one with the Gentiles. Now, isn't that something?

"But, you know, we found that being one with Christ had some other implications. It also meant, for all of us—Jew and Gentile believers—that we would witness to the reality and power of Jesus Christ and his oneness with God. And, given the world in which we live, that meant trouble! Our oneness with him meant that we, too, came to know what it meant to be ridiculed and persecuted because we too tried to live by what he had taught us. Even worse, many of us were killed in terrible ways. We came to know oneness in Christ through our suffering.

"Sometimes the way seemed a fiery trial. Sometimes, well . . . I wonder: Do you, living in your time, realize that Jesus was praying for you, too? He was, you know. Do you have any idea what it means if this prayer is answered for you and you become one with one another and with him? Maybe you ought to try to find out."

SUGGESTIONS FOR WORSHIP

Call to Worship (John 17 adapted)

LEADER: And this is eternal life

PEOPLE: That we know God and Jesus Christ whom God has sent

LEADER: For Jesus Christ made God's name known to us

PEOPLE: That the love of God may be in us

ALL: And that we may be one.

Prayer of Confession

We are not skilled at creating unity, O God. We are not talented at sharing your love. When we rely on our own tendencies, abilities, and preferences we get in trouble. Unity does not come naturally to us. Forgive us, fill us, and teach us, O God. For we pray in Jesus' name. Amen.

Assurance of Pardon

Who is in a position to condemn?
Only Christ and Christ died for us,

Christ was raised for us,
Christ *prays* for us.

Benediction (I Pet. 5:10)

The God of all grace, who has called you to eternal glory in Christ, restore you, establish you, and strengthen you.

Day of Pentecost

Joanna M. Adams

Numbers 11:24-30: The resting of the spirit on the chosen elders and on Eldad and Medad who had remained in the camp.

Acts 2:1-21: Scripture's record of the disciples' and the crowd's experiences on Pentecost from the coming of the Holy Spirit to the beginning of Peter's sermon.

Psalm 104:24-34, 35*b*: A psalm of praise to God as the One who creates and sustains the world.

I Corinthians 12:3*b*-13: Paul's description of the diverse gifts of the Spirit in the Christian community and the unity of all Christians in Christ.

John 20:19-23: The experiences of the disciples Easter night.

John 7:37-39: Jesus' words about the promised Spirit gushing from the believer's heart like a river of living water.

REFLECTIONS

Recently, I heard the administrator of a large city hospital say that the first thing she does when she arrives at the office in the morning is to ask her secretary, "What's new?" The secretary usually has an answer, one different from the day before. The breathtaking changes in health care are emblematic of the age in which we live. There are winds of change blowing across virtually every aspect of modern society: politics, economics, communication, business, and industry. That same hospital administrator told of her husband who has worked for the same corporation for twenty years, but in those twenty years the company has been sold five different times. Change is in the air. The rapidity of its pace is increasing. The current rate of technological change alone is enough to take your breath away. I heard one corporate executive say recently that in his own industry, between 25 percent and 40 percent of the technology the industry is now using will become obsolete within the next twelve months.

We have already arrived at the point at which some statistics show that more computers than televisions are being sold every year. Amazing. I vividly remember that magic day in 1953 when my father brought home our first television set. On warm summer evenings we would turn the window fan down low, turn off the lights in the living room, and watch with rapture whatever was being shown on WTOK-TV. Sometimes it would be Teresa Brewer in a white dress, belting out a song. Sometimes there would be trouble at the station, and we would get only the test pattern. We watched that, too. The memories seem quaint as we close in on the end of the twentieth century. As close as we are now to the doorway that leads to the new millennium, there will be no way to avoid the mighty breath of the future that is blowing in.

In May 1996 on Mount Everest the wind blew so ferociously that experienced and sure-footed climbers were knocked off their feet, became disoriented, and lost their way. Some even lost their lives.

Is there a way for our world to keep its grounding in the midst of turbulent times?

A Sermon Brief

The Scriptures of our tradition speak of a force at work in the world, an invisible power that is compared to breath and wind. The first chapter of the first book of the Bible names this creative force "God." "In the beginning when God created the heavens and the earth, the earth was a formless void, and darkness covered the face of the deep, while a wind from God swept over the face of the waters" (Gen. 1:1-2).

And when the human creature was created, formed from the dust of the ground, God breathed into that creature's nostrils the breath of life.

Consider this. Consider that as it was in the beginning, so it is also now. Consider that the Spirit of the living God is hovering still over this world. Consider that into any lifeless, hopeless human spirit, one that is sagging with weariness or paralyzed with fear, the Holy Spirit still will breathe life and peace, if only the human creature has the sense to receive the Holy Spirit.

It is a strange day, this Pentecost Sunday. Christian churches around the world pause to draw in a breath of fresh air as they celebrate the gift of new life to the church. But according to all the stories that our faith tradition tells, it is not just the church that receives life-giving power from above. Nor is the Spirit held in reserve and doled out only to a select few, like Moses or Mother Teresa. The Spirit is given generously and freely to all who will receive it.

One of the clichés currently in vogue in our contemporary speech is to say that a creative person is somebody who is willing to "color outside the lines." God was the one who had that concept originally. In the wilderness the Spirit rested upon two surprising people, Eldad and Medad, who hadn't even gone to the tent meeting that day. "But the spirit rested on them" (Num. 11:26), and they were thereby given the gift of prophesying, which is nothing more or less than the willingness to step out, to scout out the future, and come back and tell the others "I have looked, and this is the way God would have us go." Those touched by the Spirit declare, "Let us go forward with God."

But the Israelites wanted to turn back. I understand. Many in our day have a similar longing in the midst of the tumultuous changes around us. Let's go back and do it the way we used to do it. Remember the good old days. Give us old-time religion. Remember when Cokes used to cost a nickel and a movie ticket was twenty-five cents? When life was simple and the answers were easy? Every time I begin to get nostalgic about the fifties, the era in which I grew up, I make myself remember that it wasn't so swell for everyone. What if I had been a little Black girl growing up where I grew up? When I got on the bus to go downtown, to go to the Temple Theater or the Royal Theater, I would have been told to sit in the back of the bus, and when I got there I couldn't even have gone to these theaters because of the color of my skin. Every time I get nostalgic about the way things were, I think about what it might have been like if I had been an adult back then. I certainly would have had to find another line of work.

If we know anything, we know that the past is past. Much of it was good. Much of it we miss. For some it was life-stifling rather than life-enhancing, but whether it was good or bad, it is behind us. The only way is the way ahead. The reason is simple: You and I are needed to participate in building the new reality that is the creation of God. As it was with the Hebrew people, we move on in the direction of tomorrow. I am not saying it is easy; I am saying that God can be trusted with the future and will give us what we need.

After Jesus' death—an earthshaking change—his disciples were unsettled and disoriented. According to John's Gospel, they locked themselves in a room. But a locked door could not keep out the Spirit of a risen Lord. He came to them and stood among them and said, "Peace be with you" (John

20:19, 21). Then he gave them his commission to enter the world and work as he had worked for its renewal. He breathed on them and said, "Receive the Holy Spirit" (John 20:22). The Spirit of God that brings life and peace—that is all any human being needs, isn't it?

Because God breathed the Spirit into him, Adam got up out of the dust. Because Jesus breathed the Spirit into them, the disciples got up and shook off their fear and went on to do what needed to be done. Certainly, the days would come when fierce winds would swirl around them, but they would not lose their footing or sense of direction. The Spirit of life, the peace of Christ, kept them steady through every storm.

The challenges human society currently faces can seem overwhelming. The sheer volume of information we must process, the frantic pace of life, the disintegration of a common set of values, the increased complexity of moral decision making—these realities tempt us to get into bed and pull the covers over us. But by the Spirit of God we can learn to live in the midst of change and do what we can for the renewal of the world. Remember God's Spirit in the first human creature; God's Spirit in Eldad, Medad, and the other elders; God's Spirit in the fear-filled disciples; God's Spirit on Pentecost Sunday. This same Spirit continues to inspire the people of God—that's you and me—to move forward into God's future.

In 1942, with Nazi Germany at war, German churchman Dietrich Bonhoeffer wrote:

One may ask whether there have ever before in human history been people with so little ground under their feet.[1]

He went on to express his Pentecost faith:

There are people who regard it as frivolous, and some Christians think it impious for anyone to hope and prepare for a better earthly future. They think that the meaning of present events is chaos, disorder, and catastrophe; and in resignation or pious escapism they surrender all responsibility for reconstruction and for future generations. It may be that the day of judgment will dawn tomorrow; in that case, we shall gladly stop working for a better future. But not before.[2]

SUGGESTIONS FOR WORSHIP

Call to Worship (Ps. 104:33, 35*b*)

LEADER: I will sing to the LORD as long as I live;

PEOPLE: I will sing praise to my God while I have being.

LEADER: Bless the LORD, O my soul.

PEOPLE: **Praise the LORD!**

Prayer of Confession

O God of Pentecost, God of the Spirit that hovers even today over the world for which Jesus died: Forgive our timidity, our fearfulness as we look around us at the world. Forgive our resistance to your Spirit that urges us to encounter the world for the sake of the gospel and not to run away. Fill us with your Holy Spirit. Grant us peace in the midst of the confusion around us. Grant us boldness that inspires us to step into the future with you.

Charge and Benediction (John 20:19, 21, 22)

Hear and believe the life-giving, peace-giving words of Jesus: Peace be with you. Peace be with you. Receive the Holy Spirit.

———————

1. Dietrich Bonhoeffer, *Letters and Papers from Prison*, ed. Eberhard Bethge (New York: Macmillan, 1971), p. 3.
2. Ibid., pp. 15-16.

Trinity Sunday

Joanna M. Adams

Genesis 1:1-2, 4*a*: The beginning of creation when a wind from God swept over the primal waters.

Psalm 8: A poetic celebration of God's creation and God's giving humans dominion over that creation.

II Corinthians 13:11-13: Paul's charge and trinitarian benediction to the church in Corinth.

Matthew 28:16-20: The disciples' commissioning to make disciples and to baptize in the name of the Trinity.

REFLECTIONS

I might as well say that while I love to study theology, doctrines as such do not do a whole lot for me.

Faith and its symbiotic soul mate, doubt, have been indispensable traveling companions in the course of my life, but a doctrine—like the Trinity—served up cold and plain without seasoning is to me like brussels sprouts for the mind. I know that brussels sprouts are full of things my body needs. I know that I ought to want to eat them when they are placed before me, and I will eat them, but they don't thrill my soul.

It is like that with doctrines. No doctrine has ever gotten me through a personal crisis or comforted me when I was afraid or filled that empty place inside of me that longs for God.

"I stretch out my hands to you; my soul thirsts for you like a parched land," the psalmist wrote in 143:6. He was not yearning for a doctrine.

We need to be realistic about our expectations where doctrines are concerned. We should not expect a theological concept to quench a spiritual thirst. Faith, love, and hope—these are the divine gifts that sustain us throughout our lives. But let us never forget that the life of the mind is a gift from God, as well. Let us not forget that theology, though it is a secondary gift, is an indispensable one. Theological concepts, called doctrines, help the church think about and give voice to the truth it knows by faith. A doctrine will keep the church from taking off on a tangent and losing its way. The Christian faith is not what individuals decide it is on any given day. It is a historically and theologically grounded means of understanding the nature of God and the mystery of the universe.

A SERMON BRIEF

On the liturgical calendar today is Trinity Sunday, a day set aside for reflecting on the one triune God, "whom alone we worship and serve," or so our most recently composed Presbyterian creed proclaims.

So what about this fundamental Christian premise of God as Trinity? Perhaps your first thought is that you cannot imagine what that means, God as Trinity. That is not an inappropriate thought.

Augustine once made this general statement: "If you think you understand it, it isn't God." The British writer Dorothy Sayers wrote that the average churchgoer is baffled specifically by the Trinity: "The Father [is] incomprehensible, the Son [is] incomprehensible, and the whole thing [is] incomprehensible."[1]

To be sure, God cannot be put in a box and tied up with a ribbon of words, but the fact that the human mind cannot fully comprehend the divine, nor can human speech explain it, does not mean that a concept about God cannot be comprehended, or that human speech cannot illumine the concept.

God is a mystery, but the idea of God as triune is a helpful, clarifying way for the church to speak about and to think about God and to name the ways God has been known and experienced by those who have gone before us.

There is no doctrine of the Trinity in the Bible, but there is evidence all across its pages that its writers and the communities for which they were writing concluded that there was but one God. "Hear, O Israel: The LORD our God is one LORD" (Deut. 6:4 RSV). This radical monotheism was the great contribution of the Hebrew people to the ancient world, a world in which it was assumed that there were many different gods competing for the loyalties of the people.

God was One, God is One, but this one God is at work in human life and in human history and the cosmos in more than one way, much as we experience another person acting in a variety of ways, according to what the situation calls for. Think about a parent over the course of a child's life. Sometimes that parent is comforting, sometimes correcting, sometimes tenderly concerned, sometimes standing strong with conviction, but it is always the same person. So it was that the people sometimes experienced God as being over them, sometimes alongside them, sometimes ahead of them in the future.

The benediction that Paul gave to his friends in Corinth named the mysterious, multifaceted reality they had come to know and worship: "The grace of the Lord Jesus Christ, the love of God, and the communion of the Holy Spirit" (2 Cor. 13:13).

It was from such benedictions, as well as hymns, sermons, and stories that the doctrine of the Trinity evolved. This doctrine over time became an indispensable theological construct through which eternal truth could be glimpsed.

The doctrine of the Trinity insists that God—divine transcendence beyond our grandest imagining—was fully revealed for all the world to see in Jesus of Nazareth. Perhaps the challenge of the Trinity to the modern mind is its strong claim that, at a particular time in history, time and eternity intersected in a unique way. In Paul's words the love of God is fully manifest in the grace of the Lord Jesus Christ. I have come across the writings of a wonderful theologian, a Lutheran named Ted Peters. He writes, "The birth of the cosmos issues from the same tender heart of God that celebrated the birth of the Messiah at Bethlehem."[2] But the doctrine of the Trinity does not stop there. It goes on to maintain that even now the Holy Spirit enters into human hearts and minds so that we can commune with the love of God and the grace of Jesus Christ. Contrary to popular opinion, hydrogen and oxygen and carbon are not the basic elements of the universe. Rather, communion with the divine, grace, and the love of God are the basic elements of the universe.

Three in One; One in Three. The Trinity seeks to describe the inexplicable and to name that love, that grace, that communion we have experienced as divine.

There is an Indian religion that dates back to the sixth century B.C., called Jainism. Its followers have a word: *syat.* They use it often in their conversations. It means "to the best of my knowledge at this time." They use it to remind themselves and others that that is all anyone has to go on: our knowledge at the time.

That might be a helpful way to think about the Trinity, remembering that for two thousand years it has served the community of faith well. Remember, though, it is only a doctrine about God. It is not God. Only God is God.

One of this century's greatest Christian thinkers, the Reverend Dr. Martin Luther King Jr., reminds us of God:

> At times we've said,
> "He's a rock in a weary land.
> He's a shelter in the time of storm."
> At times we've said that somehow he's a mother
> to the motherless and a father to the fatherless.
> At times we've just ended up saying,
> "He's my everything."[3]

SUGGESTIONS FOR WORSHIP

Call to Worship*

LEADER: What do you mean when you say the word "God"?

PEOPLE 1:   The creative force that called the cosmos into being.

PEOPLE 2:   A presence that is as close as the air we breathe, a presence and power that guide and sustain us in our daily life.

LEADER: What do you mean when you say the word "God"?

PEOPLE 1:   Jesus, son of Mary, born in a manger.

PEOPLE 2:   Yahweh, the mighty God of Moses, who spoke from a burning bush, and possessed the power to part the sea.

LEADER: What do you mean when you say the word "God"?

PEOPLE 1:   One great, divine reality to which all religions in the world bear witness.

PEOPLE 2:   The God of the Christian Gospels.

LEADER: What do you mean when you say the word "God"?

---

*Before offering the Call to Worship, divide the congregation into two groups. For example, you may use each side of the sanctuary, the choir and the congregation, women and men, those younger than thirty and those older than thirty, and so forth.

BOTH: The One whom we are here to worship.

LEADER: Let us worship God.

Prayer of Confession

O God, forgive us when your greatness, your majesty, your transcendence cause us to draw away from you and to confine you to the far-off heavens. Forgive us when our attitude toward you makes you a pal or a chum so that we expect no surprises, see no need for repentance, and experience no sanctifying transformations. Forgive us, O God, when we think we understand you too well *and* when we think you are too Other for us to understand at all. Be with us in our confusion and doubt. Be with us as presence and mystery. Be with us, for we thirst for you, our God.

Benediction (II Cor. 13:13)

The grace of the Lord Jesus Christ, the love of God, and the communion of the Holy Spirit be with all of you.

---

1. Ted Peters, *God as Trinity* (Louisville: Westminster/John Knox Press, 1993), p. 28.
2. Ibid., pp. 186-87.
3. Richard Lischer, "The Interrupted Sermon," *Interpretation* 50, no. 2 (April 1996): 176.

Ordinary Time 12 or Proper 7

Esther Hargis

Genesis 21:8-21: Abraham and Sarah cast Hagar and Ishmael out into the wilderness. God opens Hagar's eyes to the presence of a well.

Psalm 86:1-10, 16-17: A prayer for deliverance that Hagar could well have prayed.

Romans 6:1*b*-11: If we die with Christ, we will rise with him. Such dying and rising frees us from sin and death.

Matthew 10:24-39: This section of the missionary discourse has two themes: "Do not be afraid; you are of more value than many sparrows," and "Be afraid, following Jesus is a costly thing."

REFLECTIONS

The story of Hagar is not a particularly familiar story to most congregations. The Genesis passage tells of the use and abuse of Hagar by Abraham and Sarah, people of the covenant, people of faith. This story reveals the shadow side of people of faith in stark terms and serves as a warning to people of faith about their shadow side. It is a reminder of the importance of examining our actions and our attitudes both individually and systematically. This text underscores the need that people of faith have to confess and repent of their sins.

The story of Hagar also helps us to acknowledge that there are people in our communities, even in our congregations, who understand this kind of story. It validates victims' experience and places the burden on those who, by their rejections, insensitivity, and arrogance have used and abused them.

I did this sermon from Hagar's viewpoint. I walked determinedly down the aisle to the pulpit, using a scarf to create the character. "Hagar" was not hostile to the congregation, but she clearly had no illusions about them either. She certainly did not assume they were glad to see her or to hear what she had to say. But she had her say, without a hint of apology for the congregation's discomfort. When she left she walked out with dignity. She taught us the meaning of repentance.

A SERMON BRIEF

Do you know me? I'm an innocent victim of use, abuse, and rejection; I'm the exploited faithful maid; I'm the surrogate mother; the illegal alien without legal resources; the mistress; I'm the runaway; the rejected wife; the divorced mother with child. I'm the homeless woman; I'm the welfare mother, I'm the self-effacing female who has lost her identity in service to others.[1]

Do you know me? My name is Hagar. Let *me* tell you my story. Yes, I am an Egyptian slave, but not just one of many. I was Sarah's personal servant in a position of trust, a gift to her from Sarah's parents when she married Abraham. I knew her in a way no one else knew her, including Abraham. I knew Sarah's barrenness caused problems between her and Abraham. I knew how she suffered. I knew how Abraham's actions were felt as a reproach; giving Sarah to Pharaoh was cowardly of Abraham and demeaning to Sarah. I saw Sarah grow bitter toward God. Sarah's life had gotten out of her control, and yes, she was frightened. Sarah tried to get control of her life by a not uncommon practice: She sent her husband to me. Sarah's identity was defined by Abraham. She thought if I had a child by Abraham, then the child would count as her own. But it wasn't as simple as that.

There are those who say that after I conceived I looked with contempt on Sarah, but that's not true. I was just happy and wanted to share that joy with Sarah. I saw us as on equal footing —more than slave and mistress; more like sisters. But Sarah couldn't bear that. She accused me of being insolent and disrespectful. She complained to Abraham, who couldn't deal with the conflict and would do anything to avoid it. He gave in to her as he did so often, and I went from being a trusted servant to being a slave deserving of particularly harsh treatment.

I just couldn't take it, and I ran away. Beside a spring of water in the wilderness a messenger of God told me to go back and also told me that God would greatly multiply my offspring. I would bear a son whom I was to name

Ishmael. So I went back and gave birth to Ishmael and became just one more of Abraham's concubines.

In time Sarah did conceive and gave birth to Isaac, but somehow she still couldn't be happy. When Isaac was weaned, as was the custom, Abraham gave a great feast. Ishmael and Isaac were playing together, and when Sarah saw them, she just snapped. Somehow she saw Ishmael as a threat to Isaac and to her future. There certainly was no reason for her to feel this way, for God had made the covenant with *both* her and Abraham. Yet she demanded that I be banished immediately. At daybreak the next morning Abraham gave me bread and water, handed Ishmael to me, and, looking a little guilty, sent us out into the wilderness.

In a short time, the bread and water ran out. I knew we were both going to die; it was the most terrifying and agonizing moment of my life. I couldn't bear to hear Ishmael's cries. I thought I would go crazy from grief. In trying to distance myself emotionally, I distanced myself from him physically. I placed him under a bush so the hot sun would not add to his suffering, and I went as far away as I dared, so I could just see the bush on the horizon. And I wept, and I wept. . . .

But God heard our cries and showed me a well of water, and I took some to Ishmael. Ishmael seemed from that point on to thrive in the wilderness, becoming an expert with a bow. I never really got used to it, but I found him a wife from Egypt, and we made a life for ourselves. Oh no, I'm not saying we all lived happily ever after, but the harshness of the wilderness was more bearable than the abuse and cruelty of Abraham and Sarah.

Yes, there was a time when I was angry with God for the suffering we experienced. But in time I came to realize that our suffering was not because of God, but because of the sin of Abraham and Sarah, children of the covenant. It didn't have to be that way. Sarah and I could have become like sisters, and Isaac and Ishmael like brothers, without diminishing God's covenant. In fact, it would have enhanced that covenant. Abraham could have stood up to Sarah, assured her that she would no longer receive his reproach and reminded her of God's covenant. Two great peoples could have been established, living in harmony. But their jealousy, their anger, their passivity, their cruelty was the root of their sin. I was wounded for their sins; I was bruised for their iniquity.

What happened to me happened because the people of the covenant forgot what covenant means. They betrayed the covenant. There are people around the world who are like me, suffering and wounded for the sins of the people of the covenant, both old and new. The "homeless, landless, penniless, powerless, faceless, voiceless" are bruised because of the faithlessness of people of faith.[2]

In every community, countless women like me despair of their lives. In every community, the eyes of women like me still look upon their sick and dying children—in New York and Soweto, in Baghdad and Berkeley—perhaps sitting in the pew next to you or just outside the door or maybe it's your neighbor down the street. If the people of the covenant do not demonstrate gentleness and compassion, if the people of the covenant do not demand justice and peace, who will?

Do you know me? Do you even want to? My name is Hagar. My story is a story of "exodus without liberation," and upon me and my sisters is the chastisement that makes you whole.[3]

SUGGESTIONS FOR WORSHIP

Call to Worship (Ps. 86:8-13 adapted)

LEADER: There is none like you among the gods, O Lord, nor are there any works like yours.

PEOPLE: **All the nations you have made shall come and bow down before you, O Lord, and shall glorify your name.**

LEADER: For you are great and do wondrous things; you alone are God.

PEOPLE: **Teach us your way, O LORD, that we may walk in your truth; give us an undivided heart to revere your name.**

LEADER: We give thanks to you, O Lord our God, with our whole heart, and we will glorify your name forever.

UNISON: **For great is your steadfast love toward us!**

Prayer of Confession

Merciful God, we confess that we have been unfaithful to you and unloving to those around us. When those in need have cried out for help, we have turned our backs upon them, and in so doing have shut the doors of our hearts to your love for them through us. Forgive us. Amen.

Assurance of Pardon (Matt. 10:27, 30-32 adapted)

LEADER: Jesus says, "Everyone who acknowledges me before others, I will acknowledge before my Father in heaven."

PEOPLE: What Jesus taught in the dark, we will tell in the light. What we have heard in a whisper, we will proclaim from the rooftops.

LEADER: You are of great value to God; the very hairs of your head are numbered.

PEOPLE: Thanks be to God!

Benediction

Go forth as people of God's covenant. Be faithful to what that means; be courageous in living it out. And know that God's love will sustain you.

---

1. I credit Phyllis Trible's book *Texts of Terror: Literary-Feminist Readings of Biblical Narratives* for inspiring this sermon. I knew when I read this book I had to get at least one sermon out of it!
2. Mary Lou Sleevi, *Women of the Word* (Notre Dame, Ind.: Ave Maria Press, 1989), p. 30.
3. Trible, p. 4.

Ordinary Time 13 or Proper 8

Beth Merrill

Genesis 22:1-14: Abraham's faith is tested when God commands that Isaac be sacrificed. At the last minute, the angel of the Lord intervenes, resolving the dilemma.

Psalm 13: In simple words and few verses, the psalmist captures the anguish of the faithful when God seems to be absent or unresponsive. In frustration, the psalmist makes demands of God, but in the end finds acceptance in God's love, salvation, and blessing.

Romans 6:12-23: Paul continues his argument about the effects of sin and human choice. Within his stern words about the abundance of sin and the failures of human beings to break free from sin, he weaves the truth of God's grace. We have been freed, he says, and eternal life is our free gift.

Matthew 10:40-42: Jesus' admonition of hospitality echoes an earlier part of Abraham's saga: When you offer hospitality to a stranger, you may be entertaining angels—or even God—unaware. Great will be the reward of those who extend the welcoming hand.

REFLECTIONS

Today's reading from the Old Testament is one of the most troubling passages in Scripture, but to explain it away is to risk denying its power. The power of the text is expressed in God's demand and God's grace. In some ways, this passage is the culmination of the saga of Abraham and Sarah, who were promised so much, blessed so well, and now, are tested by what they hold most dear. One could do much with the four principal actors in the story: God (Elohim in this part of Genesis), who makes promises and keeps them, who asks for ultimate loyalty and trust; Abraham, destined to be the patriarch of many nations, wise and strong and obedient, desperate to be the father of a legitimate heir; Sarah, not present in the story but whose absence makes a statement about the role of women, wives, and mothers in God's plan for the chosen people; and Isaac, the one who laughs, almost an innocent victim, and a necessary link between the generation of Abraham and Sarah and the generation of Joseph.

A Sermon Brief

We've all had nightmares—dreams that never seem to end, dreams from which we seemingly cannot awaken. We've all had those dreams that take hidden worries and real events and warp them into mangled labyrinths of stories in which we, or those we love, are put into terrible situations. Eventually we awaken and the horror fades as the day goes on, but the fear rumbles on quietly—the fear that the nightmares might become reality, that we will know anguish. Nightmares are, in a sense, terrible stories that we pray will never come true.

This narrative about Abraham and Isaac is like a nightmare. It presents our God doing something that seems quite cruel. It is a terrible story, and wrangling with it makes me wonder if maybe God can ask too much of us; if God can require that we endure things that will break us; if God ever allows us to go through experiences that just might kill us. And that's an ugly picture of God. It's a picture that contradicts so much of what I believe God to be like.

It's tempting to avoid a story like this, to focus on the warm fuzzies in our Bible rather than the more bleak passages. But I reckon that some day you will wrestle with this story as it is retold in your own life. The characters may change a bit, the details switch themselves around. But some day, if it hasn't happened already, you and I will find ourselves unable to sleep at four A.M., awake to a nightmare of a situation, deciding that God has asked too much of us.

One of the best ways to cope with a nightmare is to face it head-on, to go over the details, to confront whatever in it is frightening and dismantle the fear. So let us go back to this story, and walk through it together, and face the good, the bad, and the frightening in it.

We begin with God. By the time we reach today's chapter, we learn that God has promised good to Abraham, and God has followed through. And now God has decided to test Abraham, to test his devotion, to test his trust.

Then, of course, we have Abraham, who has been very obedient and very grateful to God. He has received wealth and victory, and a son by a concubine, and then, joy of joys, a legitimate heir by his beloved and menopausal wife, Sarah. Abraham is a blessed man, and he is about to be tested. Will he trust the God who has come through on every previous promise, or will his own great love for his son create doubt?

Then we have Isaac, the promised son, old enough to carry a few logs of wood, and still young enough to trust his father. Isaac is the realization of God's promise fulfilled, and the love he has for his father is grounded in the mutual love of and by God, who gave the life of this child to his parents. And now this life is about to be compromised.

Missing from this episode is Sarah, but her absence is part of the story as well. God had promised good to Sarah too, and while Sarah had had a good chuckle at the thought of becoming a mother long after child-bearing potential, she too knew gratitude to God. Now Sarah is about to become a passive character in this terrible story, asked to trust her husband and her God with the life of her laughter.

Even before the plot thickens, questions leap up. How could Abraham be so obedient to God in what seems to be a denial of his love for Isaac? How could he look into the eyes of that trusting, laughing, miracle of a boy and ask him to go up to the mountain with him? And how could he leave on that terrible journey without a word to Sarah? Did Isaac fear? Did Sarah know that something was up? What if the angel had been delayed? Or the ram tangled up in the wrong shrub? Too many things could have gone wrong. This story could have had a terrible beginning, a terrible middle, and a terrible ending. But of course it didn't.

In his book *Messengers of God*, Elie Wiesel comments on this story about Abraham and Isaac. He says, "The miracle took place. Death was defeated, the tragedy averted. . . . Was thus the mystery resolved? Hardly. . . . It leaves one troubled. The question is no longer whether Isaac was saved but whether the miracle could happen again. And how often. And for what reasons. And at what cost."[1]

What kind of God is this who tests the people with situations that teeter on the brink of tragedy? What kind of God is this who has tested so many with situations that do become tragedies? Will this kind of God allow the miracle to happen again, in our own lives?

I don't know. There is much about God that is unknown, and that scares me. There is part of God that I fear—the omnipotence of God overwhelms me, and I fear I could be swallowed up by all that bright power.

I wonder if you can identify a fear of God that you have, if you have any at all. I would suspect that some of the fears we have about God are quite common—that God will desert us, that God will allow us to suffer, that God will test our trust in some terrible, wrenching way. Many have faced those same fears.

What do we make of a God who can grant us both blessing and curse, both presence and absence? How do we live with the paradox of trusting God and knowing that same trust leaves us all so very vulnerable to God? How do we live with the love and the fear? How can we trust?

Trust requires that we make a choice without having all the facts before us. Still, it is a human tendency to hedge our bets a bit, and so we move into the relationship of trust with God with our eyes as wide open as they can be.

We remind ourselves that God's ways are not our ways, and that God has the power to give and take life. We remind ourselves that our devotion to God will require more than we think we can give at times. And we remind ourselves of all the promises God has kept, and of all the blessings we have known. We, like Abraham, are asked to trust that whatever fear we have of God cannot possibly overcome God's love for us.

Easier said than done, I know. But I know some of you, and I know you have endured tragedies that I pray I will never know, and yet here you are, in church, worshiping God; here sometimes in faith and sometimes in doubt; here to offer God thankfulness one day and anger another. But you are here, and your presence is a testimony to the fact that nothing can overwhelm divine love. And I thank you, beyond my ability to express it, for showing me that truth again and again. Thanks be to God. Amen.

Suggestions for Worship

Call to Worship

LEADER: We gather to worship our God.

PEOPLE: **We sing to our Divine Creator, the One who has dealt bountifully with us.**

LEADER: Now is the time to approach God with honesty, and with fear, and with love.

PEOPLE: **We praise the God who asks much of us. We praise the God who blesses us.**

LEADER: With joyful and awestruck hearts, let us worship God.

Prayer of Confession

Great and loving God, who are we that you are mindful of us? You are the One who makes promises; you are the One who keeps those promises. We hear your words and doubt their truth; we see signs of your grace all around us, and still we pretend we are blind. You have the power to annihilate us, but again and again you offer us life. We cower in weak fear, sensing that it is easier to believe that we are meaningless entities rather than heirs of your promise. Forgive us, O God, and redeem us. Amen.

Assurance of Pardon

Sisters and brothers, this is the promise that God has fulfilled in Jesus Christ: Your sins are forgiven. Believe this in your hearts, and be at peace. Alleluia! Amen.

Benediction

Aware of your fears, assured of God's love, go now in peace. And may the love of God sustain you this day and always, through Jesus Christ our Savior. Amen.

---

1. Elie Wiesel, *Messengers of God: Biblical Portraits and Legends* (New York: Random House, 1976), p. 73.

Ordinary Time 14 or Proper 9

Mary Donovan Turner

Genesis 24:34-38, 42-49, 58-67: Abraham sends his servant to his homeland to find a suitable wife for his son. The servant finds Rebekah, and she travels to a foreign land to marry Isaac.

Psalm 45:10-17: The verses are addressed to the king who is handsome and has been blessed by God. This is a song for his wedding.

Romans 7:15-25*a*: "I do not understand my own actions. For I do not do what I want, but I do the very thing I hate." Only Jesus Christ can rescue us from this kind of sin.

Matthew 11:16-19, 25-30: Jesus prays to God in thanksgiving. His relationship to God is as child to parent. The invitation is made, "Come to me, all you that are weary and are carrying heavy burdens, and I will give you rest. . . . My yoke is easy, and my burden is light."

REFLECTIONS

The interpretation of the stories about Rebekah in the book of Genesis has had an interesting and cyclical history. In early Jewish interpretation Rebekah and other matriarchs were afforded the utmost respect. Rebekah herself is described as a matriarch, prophet, lily among thorns, blameless, and one led by an angel. Even early Christian interpretation like that of John Chrysostom (fourth century A.D.) recognized her extraordinary qualities and her willingness to risk everything for God (see the fifty-third homily on Genesis).

And yet, from these gracious beginnings, throughout the centuries the role of Rebekah in the narrative has been devalued and neglected. It seems as though there was a progressive movement to devalue the feminine. Thus, as late as the middle of this century, interpretation took an almost completely opposite stance. The stories about Rebekah deceiving her aging, blind husband led many to label her actions as discreditable and indefensible. She is seen as scheming and partisan.

Feminists now look at the stories about Rebekah with new eyes; they ask new questions. What role does Rebekah play in the Genesis narrative? How is she important in carrying on the Israelite tradition and promise? While Rebekah appears in six separate episodes in the narrative, the lectionary for the sixth Sunday after Pentecost is concerned with only the first. She appears in the story when Abraham sends his servant to Mesopotamia to find a suitable wife for his son Isaac. We know nothing about Rebekah's previous life. She appears as an answer to the servant's prayer as a suitable wife to carry on the family line. The motif of the story comes sharply into focus in Genesis 24:2b-3 when Abraham states to the servant, "Put your hand under my thigh and I will make you swear to the Lord, the God of heaven and earth that you will not take a wife for my son from the daughters of the Canaanites among whom I dwell." The goal of the story is to find the ancestress for Abraham's seed, for the future of Yahweh's people could not lie with the indigenous Canaanite people. Rebekah, then, appears as the resolution to the problem. She is the appropriate candidate to be Isaac's wife.

The idea of finding the appropriate spouse at the well is not unique to the story of Rebekah and Isaac. It is found also in Genesis 29:1-19 and Exodus 2:15-21. What is unique to this story is that Isaac, in contrast to the other prospective grooms, plays no part in the decision at all. It is Abraham's servant who finds Rebekah. And, conversely, Rebekah plays a unique role in the story in that she, in contrast to the other prospective brides, plays an active role. For while the servant and Rebekah's relatives settle the agreement for marriage, it is Rebekah who makes the ultimate decision in Genesis 24:58. "I will go," she says. And with those words she courageously decides her own fate. She is to become the shrewdest and most powerful of the matriarchs.

The succeeding account of Rebekah is parallel to that of Abraham when she receives the blessing from her family. "May you, our sister, become thousands of myriads; may your offspring gain possession of the gates of their foes" (Gen. 24:60). This blessing is reminiscent of the blessing bestowed on Abraham in Genesis 22:17. Both receive the promise of many descendants. Both shall possess the gate of their enemies. Rebekah will carry on the promise.

Her words ring out through the centuries, "I will go." And Rebekah leaves her home to travel to an unknown land, just as Abraham had done the generation before her, and just like Jacob will do in the generation to follow. The editor of the Genesis narrative wants us to remember Abraham, Rebekah, and Jacob who at great cost ventured out for their God.

A Sermon Brief

She went to the well for water, jar on her shoulder,
Unknowing that day
 that her life would be changed;
 that she would be faced with a decision;
 that she would be called upon to decide her fate.
She went to the well for water
And the servant was there,
(The servant of Abraham looking for a bride.)
 looking for the woman who would carry on the family name
 who would ensure that the blessing of God would be upon his
 family for generations to come.
She went to the well for water
As the servant said his prayer.
God of all generations, help me to find the woman who is strong
 enough to leave all the security she has, everything she knows,
 to venture forth in faith.
She went to the well for water,
And she met him there.
She gave him water to quench his thirst.
She took him home;
 not only beautiful, but compassionate she was.
Will you go? The servant asked her.
Will you go with me? I am from God.
Will you go to be the bearer of the covenant to the world?
She ran to her mother's household to tell all these things.
The others met to decide her fate.
Shall she stay?
Shall she go?
We must let her decide, they said
 and they called her forth.
Rebekah must decide for herself.
Will you go? The servant asked her.
Will you go with me, I am from God.

Will you go to be the bearer of the covenant to the world?
Like Abraham before her who left his home for the land of Canaan
Like Jacob her son who left his home for the north
Both following the call of God
Rebekah left her home.
I will go, she said.
Like women before and after her, Rebekah decided her future.
I will go, she said.
I will go.
I will go.
And her voice rings down to us through the centuries.
And the God of Abraham, Rebekah, and Jacob went with her.

SUGGESTIONS FOR WORSHIP

Call to Worship

God has called us here to listen to God's word, to sing praise, to pray. God has called us here so that we might be renewed for God's work in the world. God calls us and patiently waits to hear us say, I will go.

Pastoral Prayer (responsive)

You come to us, God, in so many surprising and unexpected ways. We know of your need for each and every one of us to respond to your calling.

Today we pray for those who are unaware of your love and embrace.

Lord, hear our prayer.

We pray for those patiently awaiting a word, a sign from you because they know they are living life with no direction, no meaning.

Lord, hear our prayer.

We pray for those who have worked and toiled their life through, often joyful, sometimes struggling under the burdens that working in your name sometimes brings.

Lord, hear our prayer.

We pray for those who are now hearing your call, those who are looking mightily for a way to respond. For those who are afraid.

Lord, hear our prayer.

We pray for those who know their calling in their heart, but who cannot find a place within the world, within the church to live it out.

Lord, hear our prayer.

For all who live and move and breathe and who are created in your powerful and gentle image we give our thanks. Amen.

Benediction

May God's spirit rest gently upon you that you might know whose you are. Amen.

Ordinary Time 18 or Proper 13

Jana L. Childers

Isaiah 55:1-5: "Ho, everyone who thirsts, come to the waters." The prophet declares that God's salvation is at hand. The passage invites God's people to feast on God's goodness.

Psalm 145:8-9, 14-21: The psalmist celebrates God's faithfulness. Not only is God "slow to anger and abounding in steadfast love" but the Lord will "give (to all) their food in due season," "satisfying the desire of every living thing."

Romans 9:1-5: Paul tells of his own grief for the Israelites. **God has elected them** and to them belong the promises of God.

Matthew 14:13-21: Jesus feeds a crowd of five thousand men, plus women and children, from only five loaves and two fish.

REFLECTIONS

The opening line of the Gospel lesson, "Now when Jesus heard this [the news], he withdrew" struck me as a hint. I was popping with questions about what was going on in Jesus' mind during the incidents recounted in Matthew 14:13-21. The exegetical sleuth in me was getting desperate. So I seized on the opening line and was promptly sucked back into the previous passage. What could cause Jesus, the Man of Compassion, to withdraw? What could cause Jesus, the Tower of Strength, to go off by himself? What could cause Jesus, the Leader of the Troops, to leave the disciples to fend for themselves?

What news had he heard? Fortunately, the question was not difficult to answer.

Rereading the story of John the Baptist's death, I was repulsed. The decadence of the dinner party and the colossal waste of the prophet's needless blood flowed together in my mind, then juxtaposed themselves against the spartan picnic scene: Waste vs. Having Enough. From there the sermon was built on New Testament scholar Herman Waetjen's insights. Jesus was reminded of his own death by his cousin's execution and all the more anxious to be sure that his disciples were equipped to carry on after he was gone, Waetjen says, so, Jesus "shows the disciples how to make use of such resources as there are."[1] *How* Jesus' example might instruct us (who know something about both waste and want) became the question for the sermon to pursue.

A SERMON BRIEF

It was a cheap and tawdry thing, as violent death sometimes is. At the end the bloody head was handed to the girl. She held it, I suppose, though it's hard to picture. Such a stupid, shocking *waste*.

In a swirl of veils, in a glint of the eye, in less time than it takes for the pork chops to be cleared and the cappuccino served, John was gone. A roaring lion, a cousin, a wild and holy man was put to an ugly death. It was a tawdry thing, and it pretty much broke up the party.

Nobody had a chance to sample the marzipan. The glasses of Madeira sat, half-full on the tables, cigarette butts floating dully near the surface. The Baked Alaska would end up in the garbage heap, with the leftover salmon and the uneaten rump roast.

The good linen cloths were rumpled, crumpled, and pushed back willy-nilly, exposing the rough boards underneath. Meaty hands grabbed on and pressed, heaving overfed bodies to their feet. The guests pushed away. The guests pushed off. The guests pushed out the door, with the grisly news on their silly, shameless lips. It didn't take long for it to reach Jesus.

"Now when he heard [the news], he withdrew," Matthew says. When he heard the story of the dinner party gone awry, the story of the little rooster of a man and his pride, the story of petty, stupid, little sins and their monumental cost—when Jesus heard the story of his cousin's ugly death, does the scripture say he cried? No. Does the scripture say he gathered his disciples around him? No. Does it say that he sent word to Elizabeth that he was on his way? No. He withdrew. The Man of Compassion withdrew from the neediness of those around him. He put his boat into the middle of the lake, and rocked on the waves.

What was he doing? Grieving, of course. Replenishing, probably. But also, I think, pondering his own vulnerability to Herod—reminded, perhaps, by the death of John the Baptist of the death that was in store for him. I think it is fair to speculate that Jesus was brought up short by John's death—it reminded him that he had a limited amount of time to do what he had to do. He had a limited amount of time to equip his disciples to take up the work after he was gone.

Jesus put ashore a sobered man—preoccupied, perhaps, with the pedagogical questions. But when the crowd pressed him, Matthew says, his compassion was kindled and he healed them. Actually, it's interesting to notice that *both* Matthew's and Mark's version of this story say that Jesus was moved to compassion by the crowds. In Matthew's story, Jesus' compassion occasions the healings; in Mark's it prompts a lecture. (On this basis alone, some seminarians have been known to establish a preference for one Gospel over the other.) Regardless of which evangelist you read, though, it is clear that Jesus was driven this time—as he was many, many times—by his compassion. Perhaps he was even driven to overcome grief, weariness, and preoccupation, to stretch himself to meet the people's needs.

Later, though, as the crowds continued to flock, and mindful of his resolve to make sure his disciples were learning how to carry on his ministry, he said to the disciples, "Here, you take it for awhile. You give them something to eat." Well they couldn't do it, could they? They couldn't manage to ease his burden even just that much, and, more to the point, they couldn't manage to show themselves to be the apt pupils that Jesus had been hoping for.

It wasn't as if they hadn't been instructed in how to do this sort of thing. They had. In fact, they'd seen the syllabus, written the required paper on mission techniques, performed passably in the classroom discussion. (You can see the course outline in Matthew 10.) But they faltered there at the point where the rubber was supposed to hit the road. "Too little resources, Lord," they said. "Our supplies are too low." "We're scraping the bottom of the barrel." "We don't have enough." And so Jesus agreed to repeat the course.

And again, instead of discoursing, philosophizing, analyzing or lecturing, Matthew's Jesus opts to teach by example. He shows them. He shows them, as Herman Waetjen puts it, how to use such resources as there are.[2]

Good, we say, our own antennae humming, as we sit forward a little in our chairs. *Oh good*, we think as we experience that feeling familiar to anyone who has ever tried to recruit Sunday school teachers, or to stretch eight pages worth of ideas to meet the minimum requirement of a twelve- to fifteen-page paper—this sounds like a good place for us to get in on this. What is the secret to learning to use such resources as there are? What do we need to know to keep keeping on in the ministry Jesus left us? What does this text have to tell us about the resource that funded Jesus' compassion—that made it possible for him to carry on an exhausting ministry to a bottomless pit of human need?

"Taking the five loaves and two fish, he looked up to heaven, and blessed and broke the loaves, and gave them to the disciples. . . . And all ate and were filled."

It's a little clue. Did you catch it? "He looked up to heaven, and *blessed* . . . the loaves." Looking up to heaven, Jesus said something like, "Blessed art thou, Jehovah, our God, King of the Universe, who brings forth bread from the earth." Looking up to heaven, Jesus performed an act of ordinary thanks—simple, mundane, predictable, quick, almost a skip-over-it-in-the-text-and-keep-going kind of thing. He thanked God and blessed the bread. And in his faith and his thanks was multiplying power.

The font that funded Jesus' ministry came out of a life of thanks. A lifetime of giving ordinary thanks. Morning by morning, evening by evening and at every meal. Walking, talking, rising, sitting. A habit, a routine, a rhythm of paying attention to God's most ordinary gifts and giving thanks for them.

Sometimes it is not so much a question of storming the throne in prayer as it is a commitment to a life of gratitude, of paying attention and giving thanks, a life of offering oneself to God.

Jesus, after all, knew the story of Elijah and the prophets of Baal. He knew how a dramatic scene was staged, about calling fire down from heaven, about getting water out of rocks, about felling the walls of the city with a prayer and a shout. He could have stormed the throne if he had wanted to. He could have mounted a spectacular, perhaps loud, perhaps public, supplication. He could have raised his arms, gone into a trance or prostrated himself before God. Be he didn't. He did the routine thing. Out of the rhythm of a life of thanks, Jesus prayed. And suddenly there was *enough*.

When I try to imagine what a life's rhythm of gratitude looks like I think of an old friend—a former teacher—and one of the best practitioners of this discipline I know. He has developed his capacity to attend to the tiny beauties of God's creation—wildflowers, hummingbirds, and praying mantis eggs; subtle colors, small shapes—the more ordinary the better, he says. He's someone who takes seriously Alice Walker's idea that God is offended when people walk right by the color purple without noticing, without appreciating. He sees things to give thanks for everywhere, he says. Dozens of things in a day—his "alleluias" he calls them. "It's the tiny alleluias that keep me going," he confided to me recently.

It's the tiny alleluias, the daily alleluias that funded Jesus' ability to use and reuse, to stretch and redouble, such resources as there are. Out of such gratitude came the spiritual resolve to see that nothing go to waste. Out of such gratitude came the spiritual power to quiet the crowd, seat them on the grass, and host a lavish, alfresco dinner party—where nobody goes away unsatisfied, and *nothing is wasted*.

SUGGESTIONS FOR WORSHIP

Call to Worship (Ps. 145:15-21 adapted)

LEADER: The eyes of all look to you, O God.

PEOPLE: **And you feed them all with a generous hand.**

LEADER: Righteous in all that you do,

PEOPLE: **You stand close to all who call, O God.**

LEADER: My mouth will speak in praise of God.

PEOPLE: **Let every creature praise God's name.**

Prayer of Confession (in unison)

Gracious God, we confess that we do not always see the gifts you have placed in our very laps. You have strewn our daily paths with beauty, but our eyes are dull; we stumble on not seeing. You have warmed our days with mercy, but our faith is cold; we go on not believing. You have filled our night with ease, but we lie down with anxiety and wake unrefreshed. Seize us, O God, we pray, and blow through us like a fresh salt breeze. Open us to your Spirit working in and among us. And teach us to praise. In the name of Jesus Christ our Lord, our example, our Redeemer, we pray. Amen.

Assurance of Pardon (based on Ps. 145:8)

LEADER: God is gracious and full of mercy, slow to anger and abounding in love. Friends, believe the Good News.

PEOPLE: **In Jesus Christ, we are forgiven. Alleluia! Amen!**

Benediction (based on Ps. 145:16, 20)

The Lord watches over all who love God and feeds us all with a generous hand.

----

1. Herman C. Waetjen, *The Origin and Destiny of Humanness* (San Rafael, Calif.: Omega Books, 1976), p. 162.
2. Ibid.

Ordinary Time 19 or Proper 14

Diane Turner-Sharazz

Genesis 37:1-4, 12-28: The selected verses introduce Joseph and his family and tell a hair-raising story of sibling rivalry. Joseph's brothers throw him into a pit in the wilderness, then change their minds and sell him into slavery.

Psalm 105:1-6, 16-22, 45*b*: These portions of Psalm 105 call God's people to worship and extol God's faithfulness by highlighting the story of Joseph.

Romans 10:5-15: The one who believes with the heart and confesses with the mouth will be saved. God is generous to all who call upon God's name. But "how are they to hear without someone to proclaim?"

Matthew 14:22-33: The text recounts the familiar story of Jesus walking on the water and of Peter's failed attempt to follow in his footsteps.

REFLECTIONS

Our scripture from Genesis presents us with our first lengthy discussion about Joseph, son of Jacob. The full story of Joseph (Genesis 37–50) chronicles the life of one who flourishes and yet so often finds himself in the direst of circumstances. Even after all that he experiences, he is able to be faithful to God and fulfill God's purposes, despite the many obstacles. Today's passage sets up the foundation and context for what occurs later in his life.

This includes the vision in a dream, the relationship between Joseph and his father and brothers, and the major circumstances that forever changes the course of his life.

Joseph's story speaks loudly, I think, to women, to racial and ethnic minorities, and to all persons who have dared to dream, who have shared the dream with others, and as a result, have found themselves persecuted for daring to own and believe the possibility that they could live it out. The vision in the dream, as we look back upon it from the end of Joseph's story, is really a call by God to faithfully serve and fulfill God's purposes, regardless. What becomes perfectly clear in the Genesis passage, however, is that Joseph's claiming of the vision in the dream leads to obstacles, hindrances, and pitfalls that one would never have expected, but with which one has to deal if committed to the vision. The action of the brothers initiates the circumstances that change Joseph's life forever. Therefore, within this text, the reader is left holding several things in juxtaposition, and in tension: dream/vision, betrayal, and the pit.

The link between all of today's texts is the theme of recognition of God and God's purposes as supreme, the overcoming of obstacles in order to fulfill the purposes, and ultimately responding to God in faith. The psalm designated for this day, Psalm 105:1-6, 16-22, 45*b*, calls upon the congregation to praise God, to remember all that God has done, and to tell the nations about God's wonderful acts. Verses 16-22 specifically refer to God's acts that relate to Joseph and his part in fulfilling God's purposes in spite of obstacles and continual testing of his faith. Matthew 14:22-33 recounts the story of Jesus walking on the water and his faith encounter with Peter. Peter steps out, in faith, into the water at Jesus' invitation. Peter, too, walks on water, but then becomes aware of and distracted by the external storm, removes his focus from faith in the One who called him out, and begins to sink. Jesus then raises the crucial question: "You of little faith, why did you doubt?" The passage ends with the disciples turning the focus back upon Jesus, worshiping him and proclaiming, "Truly you are the Son of God." Romans 10:5-15 picks up on the theme of faith as well. More specifically, it speaks of righteousness that comes from faith, and salvation that is available to all who confess Jesus Christ as Lord and believe in their hearts that God raised him from the dead. The previous obstacle of one's status in relation to the law is no longer a hindrance. "For, 'Everyone who calls on the name of the Lord shall be saved.' "

A SERMON BRIEF

Are you where you thought you would be? Or are you in a place and circumstance in which you never thought that you would find yourself, dealing with things you never thought you'd have to deal with? There are times in which life and circumstances beyond our control place us in the most unlikely of places, and we find ourselves with sunken hearts and open, gaping mouths—and life seems to be saying to us, "*Deal with this!*" I am sure that the young man, Joseph, in our scripture, was as surprised and overwhelmed as we would be, when he found himself without recognized warning or defense, being cast into the bottom of a pit in the middle of the wilderness, and left there to "deal."

This is not the way life is supposed to be. Joseph's life, up to this point, has been what we might call "charmed." He had always been the special child. His father loved Joseph so much that he made a special robe for him. This coat, this robe so rich in ornamentation, this gorgeous garment made especially for Joseph, so wonderfully and marvelously knit together by his father's hands, is unique and so special that people, even from afar, associate that coat with Joseph. And Joseph has also been given what many of us wish we could have—a vision of what our life will be like farther down the road and around the corner. God has given him foresight into the things to come. So here we have Joseph, one who is special, one who is loved, a person who is young, gifted, and blessed, one with so much going for him. How could such a person end up in a pit?

Well, it seems that for Joseph the same things that are to his benefit are, in other ways, perceived to be his determent. For you see, this son who is favored by his father has brothers who are older than he. Their father is his father, but Joseph's mother is not their mother. And the brothers, either in perception or in reality, are not so loved and favored by the father as their younger brother.

One night, Joseph tells his brothers about the vision that had come to him in a dream. The vision, in essence, says that there will come a time in which Joseph will be in a high position and his brothers will bow down to him. This dream, which would, years later, turn out to be true and a confirmation of God's blessings, comes across to the brothers as egotistical, arrogant boasting, and the tension within the building sibling rivalry mounts. The brothers begin to scheme against Joseph. "Here comes this dreamer. Come now, let us kill him and throw him into one of the pits; then we shall say that a wild animal has devoured him, and we shall see what will become of his dreams" (Gen. 37:19-20). One brother, Reuben, said, "Let us not take his life. . . . Shed no blood; throw him into this pit here in the wilderness" (Gen. 37:22). (Reuben hopes to sneak his brother out of the pit before any harm can come to him.) So Joseph's brothers strip off his robe, his identity of special status, and throw him into a pit—a pit that was empty and had no water. Twenty hands of his brothers take hold of him and cast him into a pit. Joseph goes from being favored to being hated; from a blessing to a curse, from being on top of the world to being at the bottom.

How can life be so cruel? How can those whom we consider to be "our own"—such as our family members, our friends, our brothers and sisters in the faith—become so angry, jealous, or unreasonable that they would seek to destroy us rather than let us live out our dreams?

The scripture says that when they had cast Joseph aside, the brothers sat down to eat. It is as though seeking to destroy another is routine fare, all in a day's work. They have cast their brother into a pit as easily as one would swat away an irritating fly from in front of one's face. And now they sit down to commune together in a meal. It would be as though we, in the church, have schemed together to get rid of someone in the church because they have irritated us, hurt us, or because we just don't like them, and then we come to church on Sunday and, with no thought for what we have done to this person, come to the communion table to share in the fellowship of the bread and the wine. We sometimes, like Joseph's brothers, sit down at the "table" to eat. Do not "Joseph's brothers" realize that, though they have justifiably put Joseph in the pit, they are in the wilderness? And is it not possible that the wilderness is an even bigger pit than the one in which they have put Joseph, and they don't even recognize it?

There is a reality about being in the pit that thrusts us into a different dimension of life. Life moves from surety to uncertainty, from clarity to confusion, from control to lack of control. Joseph, the one always on top of the world, found himself at the bottom of a waterless pit, a pit so deep that he is unable to pull himself out. He is now in the darkness, isolated, stripped of his sense of special identity that was represented by his colorful garment, stripped down to his vulnerability. It is at those times that, even though we have always believed in God, even though we have always tried to trust in God, we may begin to question whether God is truly with us. We may begin to doubt and feel somehow distant from God. When we find ourselves in the pit, and realize that escape from the circumstances that have befallen us is impossible, when no one is willing to give us a single hand up or out, surely we can understand the words of the psalmist who says, "Out of the depths I cry to you, O LORD. Lord, hear my voice! Let your ears be attentive to the voice of my supplications!" (Ps. 130:1-2). If you are truly there, Lord, please hear me. Don't leave me alone in this place to perish.

Time in the pit tests our faith. It can stretch the very limits of our faith and previous assurances. It does not seem far-fetched to think that Joseph might have begun to question God. He may have even begun to question the vision that came to him in his dream. "Lord, if I am in a pit, if destruction is at the door, how then can I possibly end up doing and being what you showed me in the dream? The reality of my circumstance seems to contradict the assurance of the dream. What I see and experience does not fit with the hope that has been laid before me. Lord, I believe, but help my unbelief."

I believe that as those who have been given the privilege of knowing how Joseph's story turns out, we can gain some insight as to our own pit existence. Joseph was eventually taken out of the pit by his brothers, and sold to others who took him into a foreign land. Over the years, through many succeeding triumphs and trials, pits and palaces, Joseph came to be in the position that the dream had envisioned. And he, from the loftiness of his office, was able to be a blessing to and for his family, and for a much wider community.

Although our circumstances seem overwhelming and our fate sealed, our time in the pit is not the whole of our life. It is only a pit stop along the way. And when we consider pit stops, several pictures come to mind. Pit stops are the pull-over places on the side of the road as we travel. We can be on a leisurely trip from one place to another, or we can be in the Indianapolis 500. But whatever the journey, there is always a pit stop. And it is at the pit stop that something gets done. We have the opportunity there to let go of that which has filled us up, to check out what needs to be fixed before we can move on, and to seek out and receive that which will adjust our hindrances and nourish us for continuation.

It is often in the pit that we are brought to the crossroads of life. It is there that we can find ourselves confronted with ultimate choices. There is a true story of a woman who was confronted by an ex-boyfriend late one night as she returned home. He stated that he wanted to talk to her briefly, and asked if she would just sit in the car for a few minutes. When she got in, he drove off, taking her to a dark deserted golf course that had a wooded area in the near distance (a wilderness setting). He told her to get out of the car. When she refused, he pulled a gun on her, and she, in fear, complied. He had her walk toward the woods.

In the time that it took to walk from the car to the woods, the woman experienced a wider range of feelings than she had ever experienced at one time. She was so afraid that her knees, literally, began to knock. She was more scared than she had ever been. She began to picture the newspaper article that would be buried in a corner on a back page: "Woman's Body Found in the Woods." She knew that she was facing death and there was nothing she could do about it. In the midst of her terror, it became clear to her that the only choice that she had was death or God. The woman prayed, "Lord, help!" And immediately, a peace came upon her as none she had ever experienced.

It was at that moment that she realized that, regardless of how the circumstances turned out, that she was in God's hands and care. After an indeterminate amount of time, they reached the woods. But as they entered, there seemed to be light. Sure, a person's eyes become accustomed to the darkness and they are able to let in more light. But, in the woman's mind at that moment, there was the sense of light in the darkness. Her assailant finally spoke, and said to her, "Is there anything you want to say before I do this?" She responded, "I don't know what I've done to deserve this, but I'm not afraid." The man responded, "I can see that," and handed her the gun, asking her to shoot him. She took the gun, threw it away, and after a period of time talking, the man drove her home.

God does not leave us alone in the pit. God is ever-present. The psalmist asks the question, "Where can I go from your spirit? Or where can I flee from your presence? If I ascend to heaven, you are there; if I make my bed in Sheol, you are there. If I take the wings of the morning and settle at the farthest limits of the sea, even there your hand shall lead me, and your right hand shall hold me fast. If I say, 'Surely the darkness shall cover me, and the light around me become night,' even the darkness is not dark to you; the night is as bright as the day, for darkness is as light to you" (Ps. 139:7-12). There is no place that we can go where God is not. Whatever our circumstance, however unlikely God's presence, God is there. Whether it be facing small pits that just make us stumble, or huge circumstances that seek to cause our destruction in one way or another, we have the assurance that God will not, and has not, left us alone.

We may not know how long our pit stop will be. Nor do we always know where life will lead us. But if we put our trust in the ever-present God, if we hold onto and keep our hand in the hand of God, we can face with growing courage and peace, the journey that awaits us.

SUGGESTIONS FOR WORSHIP

Call to Worship (Ps. 105:1-5*a* adapted)

LEADER: O give thanks to the LORD, call upon God's name.

PEOPLE: Make known God's deeds among the peoples.

LEADER: Sing to the Lord, lift up praises to our God.

PEOPLE: Tell of all God's wonderful works.

LEADER: Glory in the holy name of our Savior,

PEOPLE: Let the hearts of those who seek the LORD rejoice.

LEADER: Seek the LORD and God's mighty strength;

PEOPLE: Seek God's presence continually.

LEADER: Remember the wonderful works God has done.

ALL: We acknowledge the Lord our God this day. Let us, therefore, worship the Lord and continually proclaim God's holy name.

Prayer of Confession

O God of steadfast love and faithfulness, we confess today that we have not always been steadfast toward you. When life plops us in the middle of a pit, and we find ourselves looking up from the floor of our circumstances, sometimes our faith begins to wane. When we feel lonely, isolated, and distant from you, we entertain the thought that you have moved from us. When we feel helpless in our quest to overcome, and our hopelessness reaches major proportions, we begin to doubt your ability to lift us up. We wonder if you even care. When we have moved out so far on the ledge of faith that we are just hanging by a fingernail, we need your help to regain footing on the solid ground of your assurances, forgiveness for our doubting, and your strength to carry us through. Lord, help!

Assurance of Pardon

May you find assurance that the God who is steadfast is always with us. The God who hears our confession is faithful and will forgive us of all our sin. This same forgiving God gives power to the faint, and strength to the powerless. Be assured that we who call and wait upon the Lord shall be renewed in our strength.

Benediction

Now may the God who redeems our lives from the pit, give you peace that passes all understanding, and may you walk forward, with courage, along the lighted pathway of God's service.

Ordinary Time 20 or Proper 15

Jean Alexander

Genesis 45:1-15: Joseph makes his identity known to his brothers, insisting that it was God's hand that brought him to Egypt.

Psalm 133: "How very good and pleasant it is when kindred live together in unity!"

Romans 11:1-2*a*, 29-32: God has not rejected either Israel or the Gentiles but has mercy upon all.

Matthew 15:(10-20), 21-28: (What comes out of the mouth—not what goes into the stomach—defiles a person.) A Canaanite woman asks Jesus to deliver her daughter. She argues with Jesus' refusal, and he is impressed with her faith and heals her child.

REFLECTIONS

Although the lectionary truncates the Gospel reading, I felt that to do it justice, it should be read as a whole and treated as a whole. For a congregation that can't imagine getting anywhere near the book of Leviticus or the holiness codes, this is a difficult text to interpret. I highly recommend the Everett Fox translation and commentary *The First Five Books of Moses* for its explanations of the origins of the holiness codes and their meaning for Israel.

The tension in the text seems to me to be between a desire to be "holy" on the one hand, and the self-righteousness that so often is a consequence of our attempts to be "holy," on the other. In the text, this tension is reflected in the codes that focus on outer cleanliness, and in Jesus' concern for what is inside a person's heart. Matthew is not quite as forceful as Mark's Gospel about how one resolves this tension and in preaching one should remember that Jesus also said he didn't come to abolish the law but to fulfill it. In Matthew the focus of the text seems to be a condemnation of our self-righteous efforts to be pure and right with God.

A Sermon Brief

I remember distinctly a couple of weeks ago, saying to someone that I rarely got Jehovah's Witnesses or other religious groups knocking on my door. So of course, a week ago Saturday, guess who came knocking on my door?

It had been the usual busy Saturday; sermon writing in the morning, followed by preparations for dinner and then a couple of hours of work in the yard. When the knock came on my front door, I was hot, dirty, and tired; my bones ached and I just wanted to go sit in a bathtub for a long time. When I opened the door, there were two young women, each maybe fourteen years old. They did not look like the kids I see hanging around the movie theaters in Bethesda, who try their best to look scruffy and jaded. These girls were well scrubbed. They were fresh and wholesome looking, like something out of the Bobbsey Twins. They had long hair, wore no makeup and seemed so sweet and innocent. They carried some literature with them that looked a little like some of the Sunday school material you can see in any church.

Shyly, one of them held out the book she carried so that it opened out into a large picture. It was a picture of paradise. There were animals of all kinds together with humans in a parklike setting. She held out the picture and asked in her child's voice, "Would you like to live in a place like this?"

As I stood there so many different emotions went through me. They were so young. They seemed so hopeful and innocent. I was so old, tired, hot, sweaty, and many years away from innocence. I knew there was nothing they could say to me that I could believe in. And there was nothing I could say to them that wouldn't seem mean-spirited or cynical. So finally I just smiled at them, like the grandma I am, and said, "Honey, I have my own church and I'm very active in it."

They said good-bye very sweetly and graciously as I shut the door.

"Would you like to live in a place like this?"

"Would you like to live in paradise?" Of course. Who wouldn't? Who wouldn't want to live in a world where there is no disease? Where there is no cancer to waste away the bodies of our loved ones. Who wouldn't want to live in a place of peace and harmony where people weren't always fighting about something? Who wouldn't want to live where there were no rush hour traffic jams? Can you imagine a world without politicians and political conventions every four years? Now that would be paradise!

Of course we all long for paradise. And like religious people from the beginning of time, we have tried various tactics to achieve a return to the Garden where Adam and Eve lived in innocent peace at one with God. One of these tactics was ritual purity.

In Jesus' day, some of the Jewish sects, like the Pharisees, went to great lengths to maintain ritual purity in the hope that this would overcome their separation from God and draw them nearer to God's holiness. If you want to know some of the lengths they went to, just spend this Sunday afternoon reading the holiness codes in the book of Leviticus. Not only were you supposed to wash your hands before you ate—a passage that the scribes and Pharisees are referring to in the Gospel lesson for today—but the book of Leviticus is full of things you were to do and not do in order to maintain your ritual purity before God. In chapter 11 of Leviticus there is a long list of animals, birds, and insects that the people were forbidden to eat, with instructions for what to do if you touched one and were then considered defiled. There were instructions for what to do if one of these forbidden unclean creatures fell into your cooking pot. At the end of the chapter is also this reminder of why ritual cleanliness is so important: "For I am the LORD your God; sanctify yourselves therefore, and be holy, for I am holy. You shall not defile yourselves with any swarming creature that moves on the earth. For I am the LORD who brought you up from the land of Egypt, to be your God; you shall be holy, for I am holy" (Lev. 11:44-45).

Initially there were some good reasons for all these prohibitions. There are still good reasons for washing your hands before you eat, or after you have been out in public. Some of the strict rules were health rules that were important to maintain in biblical times. Unfortunately, like many of these rules then and now, they promised what they couldn't ultimately deliver. Washing your hands won't make you holy, if what is in your heart resembles the sewer. As some of you can attest from your childhood religious traditions, abstaining from drinking and dancing or from playing cards won't make you a truly holy person if your heart is filled with jealousy, hostility, racism, sexism, or denial of sexual feelings.

Jesus is so right here. It isn't the externals that keep us separated from God, it's the internals. In Jewish understanding, the heart was the seat of thought, not the brain. They didn't know about the little gray cells. They believed the most important thing about the kind of person you were was found in the heart. In those days, as today, there were different ideas about how that inside became clean, or purified and able to be in the presence of God. Purify the outside, said the Pharisees, and the inside will follow.

Now there is some wisdom here. If you are struggling with a weight problem, you don't spend your afternoons prowling around the aisles of the supermarket. If you are trying not to drink, you don't keep alcohol in your house, or take a drink urged on you by an unknowing person. If you are struggling with sexual issues, you don't spend your time reading pornography.

The popular expression "garbage in, garbage out" is a shorthand reminder that if you put nothing but garbage into your body, or into your mind, that is what is going to come out. If all you read is murder mysteries and bloody thrillers; if all you watch on TV is talk-show trash; if all you eat is junk food; if all you think about day after day is how your neighbor is a jerk, and everyone who is a different race is not to be trusted, you are going to have a malnourished, unclean spirit inside of you.

Unfortunately, what happens when you try to manage internal reality by imposing a rigid external structure is that it very often creates the opposite from what you intended. Jesus was absolutely correct when he said that what defiles us is not dirty hands, but evil intentions, adultery, theft, lying, and slander. You can withdraw from the world like the Amish and other religious groups do, and still not have a clean heart. You can eat right, read only books approved by the Christian Coalition, obey every one of the Ten Commandments, and your heart can still be full of those things that keep us from holiness.

There is a kind of self-righteousness that happens when we try too hard to be clean, when we try too hard to earn God's love, that separates us even farther from the love of God. It is like some of those overdecorated houses with the white carpets. They look beautiful in the magazine, but you wouldn't want to live there. You would always be worried about tracking in dirt. You could never relax and be yourself. You couldn't have a party with friends and laugh together, because someone might spill food on that carpet.

What worries me today almost as much as the degeneration of public culture, is those who would reinstitute a kind of new Puritanism as though it would solve all our problems. Unfortunately the kind of repression that so characterizes Puritanism doesn't lead to the kind of generous, loving-kindness or the kind of holiness we so long for. What we are to put into our hearts, with God's help, is forgiveness, joy, love, hope, all the fruits of the spirit. We do this not by withdrawing from the world, but by engaging it with the same kind of generosity of spirit that characterized Jesus.

This was really brought home to me this week in a personal way. I spent Tuesday afternoon in the Bethesda Cares office, our outreach center for the homeless in Bethesda. I was to be present while the new executive director was on vacation. I met Hugo, the new outreach worker, a clinical psychologist, and an immigrant from Peru. Neat guy. There was the usual assortment of folks and the office was jumping. There was also a family with three children, two boys ages two and three and a baby about eight months of age. The three adults and the children had lived in a tiny car for four months before they came to Bethesda Cares to get some help. The two little boys ran around the office playing with whatever got their attention. They were nice little guys and well scrubbed even though their clothes were filthy. At about four o'clock I hoisted the two-year-old into my lap. Instinctively I started rocking a bit, and the little guy went right to sleep. I held him until the office closed and meditated on what life must be like for this child. I could only pray that the interventions of Bethesda Cares would help stabilize his life and give him a chance at what we all want for our children.

When I got home that afternoon I went immediately to the bathroom and washed my hands. My pants were covered with chocolate stains that must have come from the candy bar that the two-year-old had been eating at one point in the afternoon. Street life for adults and for children is a filthy, dirty existence, far removed from our safe, middle-class lives.

It would be easy to be judgmental of the folks in that room. It would be easy to judge the choices they have made and condemn them for certain behaviors. Yet what will transform their lives and life for that child is not our judgment, but our love and compassion. For what is essential is not the chocolate stains and the grubby hands and clothes, but the open, trusting heart of a child, who can fall safely asleep in the arms of a total stranger. Even a stranger who would have much preferred not to get her hands or her pants dirty.

SUGGESTIONS FOR WORSHIP

Call to Worship

LEADER: How pleasant it is when God's people dwell together in unity.

PEOPLE: **It is like precious oil poured out on the head.**

LEADER: It is like the dew that falls on the mountains of Zion.

PEOPLE: **The unity of God's people is like the most pleasant of fragrances; the most refreshing mountain stream.**

ALL: **Let us worship God!**

Prayer of Confession

Gracious God, we confess that we long for paradise. For lands of fragrant oils and refreshing streams. We would like to live in peace with one another and with you, but we would like for it to be simple. We would like for it to happen now. We confess to you, O God, that we are tired of waiting and weary in believing. Forgive us, we pray, and show us your way to live together. In the name of Jesus Christ. Amen.

Assurance of Pardon

How we love to hang on to the past! We get all tied up remembering, keeping count, bearing grudges. God doesn't. Your past is accepted. Let it go. Live in the freedom God hands to you afresh each day. Thanks be to God.

Ordinary Time 24 or Proper 19

Amy Miracle

Exodus 14:19-31: God tells Moses to raise his hand over the Red Sea. The sea parts and the Israelites pass through it on dry ground. The Egyptian army, which has been pursuing them, is drowned when the waters return and cover their chariots.

Psalm 114: A celebration of God's work at the Exodus: "When Israel went out from Egypt . . . the sea looked and fled."

Romans 14:1-12: Paul addresses the conflict between the supervigilant members of the Christian community who meticulously observe dietary laws and special days of the religious calendar and those who believe that Christianity implies a freedom from such regulations. "Why do you pass judgment on your brother or sister? . . . Each of us will be accountable to God."

Matthew 18:21-35: The parable of the unforgiving servant. In answer to Peter's question about how many times he should forgive someone who crosses him, Jesus tells the story of a servant who harshly demanded repayment of a small debt, even though he himself had just been forgiven payment of an astronomical sum.

REFLECTIONS

I have never been very good at coloring inside the lines. On this Sunday, I strongly recommend that while we honor the lectionary's themes, we step outside the lines a bit. It is a great disappointment that the plague narrative is missing from the lectionary readings. I suggest that today's Old Testament lesson be expanded to include the whole story of Israel's liberation from bondage in Egypt. Since the entire plague narrative is too long to be read, I suggest that excerpts of the story be interspersed into the sermon. I am indebted to Walter Brueggemann for my understanding of this section of Exodus. He views the plague cycle as a rehearsal for liberation—a story told and retold to remind listeners that God and not Pharaoh is in charge.

God was willing to do whatever it took to free the Israelites from slavery. But his purpose was larger than that. The plagues were the process by which both Israel and the Pharaoh came to know the Lord. They came to know one who follows through on his intentions, who hates slavery, who breaks the laws of nature and morality to achieve his purpose.

This sermon attempts to answer the question, How would our lives be different if we thought God and not the powers of this world define what is possible?

A SERMON BRIEF

The Israelites had been forced into slavery to support the ever expanding Egyptian economy. A new pharaoh came to power and the people were no longer silent. They groaned and cried out. But they didn't cry out to the Lord for one simple reason. They didn't yet know him. But their cry for help did rise up to God. God heard their groaning, and remembered them and found a human agent to help in the work of liberation. Moses was chosen and he and his brother Aaron were sent to confront the pharaoh. The first encounter did not go well. *(Read Exod. 5:1-2.)*

Pharaoh's response was unambiguous. "The Lord? Never heard of him." Pharaoh interpreted Moses' request as an indication that the Israelites had too much time on their hands so he gave them more work to do. Not surprisingly, this did not improve the Lord's reputation with the Israelites and the Lord told Moses and Aaron to explain to the people who he was. *(Read Exod. 6:6-7a, 9.)*

The people did not yet trust this Lord. They still did not know the Lord, but they sure knew Pharaoh. They feared him, because he had so much power over their lives. It was this pharaoh that Moses and Aaron took on. In one of the most lopsided contests in history, two slaves confronted the most powerful man in the world. And Pharaoh was not alone; he was surrounded by a group of supporters: wise men and sorcerers. They were like presidential advisors; vice presidents to the Pharaoh's CEO; people who pledged their allegiance to whoever was in power.

In the first round of this contest, Moses and Aaron caused the water of Egypt to turn to blood. In a most interesting turn of events, Pharaoh's magicians duplicated their efforts and also turned Egyptian water into blood. You have to question the intelligence of a leader who would poison his own water supply to prove a point! But make a point he did. This God, the Lord, was no more powerful than the magicians. "Let your people go? Certainly not."

On to the second plague, my personal favorite, the frogs. Moses and Aaron promised Pharaoh frogs galore. *(Read Exod. 8:3-4.)*

Pharaoh's magicians could produce frogs as well, but they couldn't reverse the process. So Pharaoh went to Moses and said "Pray to the LORD to take away the frogs" (Exod. 8:8). A short time before, Pharaoh didn't know this God. Moses did pray to the Lord on Pharaoh's behalf and the frogs all died. Who says God doesn't have a sense of humor? The Egyptians were left with a huge cleanup job with dead frogs everywhere. The text says, "They gathered them together in heaps, and the land stank."

The plagues continued with gnats. The magicians could not duplicate this wonder and they said they saw the finger of God. But their boss was unconvinced. So the plagues continued: flies, then pestilence, then boils, then hail. The hail shattered every plant and every tree in Egypt, except in Goshen where the Israelites lived.

After the hail came locusts. By this time, the men around the pharaoh were begging him to give in to the Lord and let the people go. But Pharaoh's heart was hardened and there were two more plagues, first a dense darkness that covered the land for three days and then one final, horrible plague: the death of the firstborn child of every Egyptian family. *(Read Exod. 12:30-32.)*

The people were free from slavery; they were free to worship the Lord. But at what a cost to the Egyptians and to creation. Why? Why all the plagues, all the destruction, why the slow, painful defeat of the pharaoh? The answer is found in the text. God told Moses and Aaron the reason why this confrontation was necessary. "That you may tell your children and grandchildren how I have made fools of the Egyptians and what signs I have done among them—so that you may know that I am the LORD" (Exod. 10:2).

The Lord didn't just defeat Pharaoh; Pharaoh was humiliated, made to look the fool. So that generation after generation of little girls and boys could hear this story and laugh at Pharaoh. So that they would grow up to challenge the pharaohs of their day. It is no wonder that the story of the Exodus has been a favorite of oppressed people throughout the centuries. This story turns a frightening tyrant into a ridiculous fool and asserts in bold language that God and God alone defines what is just and what is possible.

Oh, Pharaoh *thought* that was his role. He believed that he and he alone controlled the destiny of the Israelites. He lost his eldest son discovering that he was wrong. The story is a gradual diminishing of Pharaoh—in the beginning, he has the power of life and death. As the plagues progress, he grows smaller and smaller until he is the only man in Egypt who believes in his power.

Who defines what is possible? Do the pharaohs of this world? Does God?

My faith tells me that God is in control, but the world tells me something different. The Congress of the United States defines what is possible. A small group of multinational corporations determine the playing field. Our human institutions and systems set limits on what can be achieved; the legal system, the economy, our political system—they define what is possible.

But then I think of this story of Moses and Pharaoh and strange images come to mind. Bill Clinton swatting away thousands of gnats. Rupert Murdoch, Bill Gates, and Donald Trump dodging baseball-size hail. Newt Gingrich knee-deep in frogs. Those men and the institutions they represent do not control our lives or define what is possible for us. That job belongs to God. Just imagine how different our lives would be if we lived them according to that truth. Think of the freedom, think of the possibilities.

I give you as an example a man named Millard Fuller. He has this crazy notion that God desires an abundant life for all people and that abundant life includes a safe place to live. He actually believes that it's possible to build enough housing so that every human being on the planet has a safe, warm place to call home. I wonder how many people have told him that is impossible and how many times he has answered back that nothing is impossible with God. Fuller is the founder of Habitat for Humanity, which in a few more years will be the largest producer of single-family housing in the United States, and the concept is rapidly spreading across the world.

What this text does more than anything else is give us permission to dream—to dream of a world where no one abuses their power, a world without pharaohs, a world where abundant life is within reach of every child. Just think of the possibilities. What the empire deems impossible is possible with God. If God and God alone sets our boundaries, just think what we can accomplish as individuals and as a community. Imagine what we here at Central Presbyterian Church could do. We could become a leading builder of low-cost housing in Denver, or dramatically expand our services to children at risk. Every room of this building could be filled with activity every hour of every day of the week. Impossible, you say?

Who defines what is possible? Amen.

SUGGESTIONS FOR WORSHIP

Call to Worship (based on Psalm 103)

LEADER: With all that is within us, let us bless God,

PEOPLE: Who forgives us all our sins, who heals all our diseases,

LEADER: Who lifts us up from rock bottom, who crowns us with steadfast love and mercy.

PEOPLE: With all that is within us, let us give praise and thanks to God!

Prayer of Confession (in unison)

We say that you are the Lord and then we live our lives as though you have no power. We bow before the powers of this world. We lack the imagination to envision a world ruled by your love. Deliver us, O God, from our limited perception. Capture the imaginations of our hearts and the work of our hands.

Assurance of Pardon

All things are possible with God. In Jesus Christ, we are forgiven!

Benediction

God and God alone defines what is possible. May your life, your work, your words, your witness be shaped by that truth! All things are possible with God!

Ordinary Time 26 or Proper 21

Beth Merrill

Exodus 17:1-17: Moses endured much during the forty years in the wilderness, including the people's complaints and lack of trust. But Moses was chosen and empowered by God to provide all things necessary for the congregation of Israel. When they were thirsty, water came; when in battle, victory was achieved. Moses set the example for God's people in obedience to God.

Psalm 78:1-4, 12-16: The excerpted verses from Psalm 78 tie together the Old Testament and Gospel lessons. The psalmist readies the people to hear a parable from the olden days passed on, and then recalls the story of the people's thirst being met by their God.

Philippians 2:1-13: Many scholars believe that the main part of this text, known as the Christ Hymn, is a quotation by Paul of an early church liturgical text. Most commentaries have in-depth analysis of the hymn.

Matthew 21:23-32: This pericope from Matthew, a saying of Jesus and a parable, makes an interesting companion to the Christ Hymn in Philippians. The Matthean text alludes to what the hymn says outright: What is the origin of Jesus the Christ, and what does obedience to God entail? The priests and elders wanted a clarification. Jesus wanted them to wrestle with the question of identity.

REFLECTIONS

There are many directions to go with the Philippians text. I chose to focus on the definition of humility as presented by the hymn; humility as the absence of selfish ambition or conceit, as regarding others as better than oneself. The image of emptying oneself and taking on the form of a slave is particularly powerful in the hymn. From that the question emerges: What does humility mean for us Christians in the late-twentieth century, especially in a country where ambition and looking out for number one are such valued qualities? And what happens in a society where there is a discernible lack of humility?

While we are all equally loved creatures and children of God, it seems that the challenge of humility differs between men and women. Little boys are taught to be aggressive, to take what they want, to overpower those weaker than themselves. Little girls are taught to be passive, to let someone else go ahead. As adults we often emerge as men of hubris and women of low self-esteem. There is a danger, of course, in getting too psychological with the idea of humility, but the preacher should be aware of the difference between humility and self-worth in the lives of the congregation.

A SERMON BRIEF

It seems that almost every day we read about another species threatened by extinction, victims of ecological changes or genetic flaws or, all too often, victims of human greed and unsportsmanship. But the animal kingdom is not the only one threatened by extinction. With society changing as rapidly as it is, with technology outsprinting ethics and morality, I fear we are in danger of losing some of our most precious virtues, and perhaps especially the virtue of *humility*.

Now we Christians play at being humble all the time, whenever we bow our heads in prayer or kneel in worship. Outside of church we deflect a compliment, or ascribe praise to someone else. But is humility merely a motion we go through, or is it a quality we aspire to incorporate into all that we are and all that we do?

In reading the passage from Philippians, I was struck by Paul's and the hymnwriter's use of "humility." Both put an emphasis on humility as the defining characteristic of the One whom we worship, and on the call for us to be in the same mind as that One, Christ Jesus. This text is about Christ's surrender to God's will, and the pain and the joy that resulted for him, and the call to Christ's followers to experience the same humility.

But before saying what humility is, it's important to say what it is not. Humility is not negation of self. It is not a sense of worthlessness. Again and again in Scripture we are reminded that humankind was created in God's image, a little lower than angels, children of God beloved by their Creator. Feeling worthless about oneself may be as big an affront to God as any of the seven vices.

Nor is humility a false lack of pride. If Michael Jordan were to say that he's just lucky most of the time, he would not be acting humbly, he would be lying. If you were to congratulate Jessye Norman after a performance, and if she were to say, "oh, it was nothing," she would not be acting humbly, but I think rather coyly. Humility is not disowning one's God-given talents and abilities.

For the Christian, humility is not an individual virtue at all. It's not a trait of the personality. It's not an internal and private attitude. In Christian terms, humility is about how we relate to one another, how we treat one another, how we balance our own self-worth with our ideas about another's worth.

Humility is about leveling mountains and lifting up valleys, and it goes deeper than our own nation's tenet that all men and women are created equal. Humility for the Christian says that equality in God's sight is valid not only for us Americans, but for the enemies of America too. The Sunday school song rings true: "Jesus loves the little children, all the children of the world. Red, brown, yellow, black and white, they are precious in his sight; Jesus loves the little children of the world."

Of course, Jesus could love anybody, and children are a lot easier to love than most adults, and the human ability to love has its limits. We can love the vulnerable, including children, because they don't threaten us, and we're willing to love another as long as it doesn't cost us too much. But love as humbly serving another? Love as regarding others as better than ourselves?

Who wants to do that? Let's be truthful: The drunk who hangs around the parking lot begging for change seems hardly worthy to shine our shoes, and is not "better" than you or me. We might pity him, feel sympathy or empathy for him, give him a dollar or point him to a food line or detox program, but regard him as better than us?

That is what God asks of us. God says to us, Yes, you might not think that this man is worthy to shine your shoes, but I am asking you to wash his feet. That is what God asks of us; that is what God asked of Jesus Christ. And that's what Jesus did.

A few years ago, a friend of mine invited me to a party he was having. I was definitely more apprehensive than my friend about the whole thing, because I knew something that my friend didn't: He was a very unconventional person, and while he was—and still is—a great friend, he did some things that were just downright bizarre, that made some people keep their distance from him.

My first cause for apprehension was the guest list. You know how some people plan a party and invite folks that they're sure won't get along, just to see what happens? My friend invented this strategy. The guest list reminded me of Halloween meets Disney, with Gloria Steinem and Pat Robertson thrown in.

Then there was the invitation. All it said was a day and a place and a general time—come around sevenish, or whenever. Nothing about what to wear or what to bring. No RSVP. I told my friend that he couldn't properly plan a party without having some knowns—such as how many people were coming—but he ignored my criticism. In fact, he laughed at my fears.

The morning of the party I awoke with my stomach in knots. I felt like I had taken on the responsibility for worrying about all the potential (and very likely) disasters of this party, and boy oh boy, was my gut ever paying for it. Granted, my friend never asked me to do this; in fact, the only thing he had asked of me was to come to the party.

Then I went through the pre-party ritual of trying on several different outfits until finally I was so tired of changing clothes that I didn't care what I looked like. I debated whether to bring a bottle of wine, flowers, or homemade bread, and ended up taking all three. I agonized over whether to arrive early to help my friend be hospitable, or to arrive late and avoid any responsibility for the disaster I was sure I would walk into. Compromise seemed the best answer, so I arrived around eight.

To this day, it remains the best party I have ever attended in my whole life. Even before I got to the door, I heard the music playing. The process of self-selection must have been operative, determining who would end up at this party, because when I walked into his very crowded home, I heard more laughter and saw more warmth and joy and fun than I had thought possible.

There was a college acquaintance—at that time an investment banker—joking it up with someone I recognized from a homeless shelter. Clustered around the onion dip were representatives of organizations that had stood on the opposite sides of a picket line just weeks before. Over in two armchairs pulled together side by side were a teenager I knew from the youth group and a resident of a retirement home, snapping their fingers and sort of dancing along to the music.

Now I much prefer to host a party than be a guest at one because that way I can attend to the ice and the stereo rather than talk to strangers. But there was my friend, working the room like the best of them, making eye contact with every guest, hugging them and clapping them on the back and offering food or drink.

I was so curious about how it all managed to work that I stayed around afterward to help clean up. We were in the kitchen, scraping dishes and sorting out the recycling, both a little quiet. Finally I turned to my friend and said, "How did you do it? How did you pull off this impossible party? It was great."

At first he didn't answer me, but just kept on sorting cans and bottles. Then at last he stopped what he was doing, looked me straight in the eye, and said, "I had a party because I wanted to share a good time with the people I care about. It didn't matter to me what anybody wore, or brought, or if they RSVP'd or not. I didn't worry about having enough to eat or drink because those things usually work themselves out. I wanted the people I love to meet one another, and to get to know one another, and I trusted them to get along, if only for my sake. I just wanted to see everyone that I cared about, and to tell them and show them that I loved them. Everything else was incidental."

I've never forgotten his words. I now live too far away to easily get to one of his parties, but I'd be there in a heartbeat if I could. And that whole experience has made me a little less anxious when I throw a party, and it's certainly made me think about who I would invite. I do know this: The next time my friend throws a party, I'd want every one of you to be there.

SUGGESTIONS FOR WORSHIP

Call to Worship

LEADER: Let all in heaven and on earth know the truth! We bend our knees and bow our heads and together we proclaim:

PEOPLE: **Jesus Christ is Lord!**

LEADER: Glory be to God who has made all things possible.

PEOPLE: **With reverence and humility, let us worship God.**

Prayer of Confession

LEADER: O Lord our God, you are wise;

PEOPLE: **You know our thoughts before we reveal them to you.**

LEADER: O Lord our God, you are compassionate;

PEOPLE: **You know our joys and fears before we name them to you.**

LEADER: O Lord our God, you are just;

PEOPLE: **You offer us mercy while we cringe at the expectation of judgment and punishment.**

LEADER: O Lord our God, you welcome every one of us;

PEOPLE: In spite of our weaknesses, our failures, our doubts, you invite each one of us into your presence.

ALL: We praise you and humble ourselves before you, O Lord our God. Amen.

Assurance of Pardon

The truth of the gospel is this: Christ came into the world not to condemn the world, but in order that the world might be saved by him. You are forgiven. Alleluia! Amen.

Benediction

Go now in peace; serve one another with joy; and may God's richest blessings accompany you wherever your path may lie.

Reign of Christ

Susan Halcomb Craig

Ezekiel 34:11-16, 20-24: God will search out and care for the lost sheep of Israel, separating the fat from the lean sheep.

Psalm 100: This famous hymn calls all the lands to praise the Lord.

Ephesians 1:15-23: Christ has been made to sit at God's right hand and God has put all things under his feet.

Matthew 25:31-46: The Son of Man separates the sheep and the goats at the great judgment.

REFLECTIONS

This Gospel story is a familiar, beloved text that immediately precedes the story of Jesus' passion. The text speaks about judgment between sheep and goats, and about the necessity of ministering with and to the hungry, naked, ill, and imprisoned. It has served over time as an urtext—a kind of life focus—for many of the saints we most admire, and a lot of the rest of us, too. It's a summary statement from Jesus' Last Discourse—like his Last Lecture— telling what's most important for us to remember from Jesus' life and teaching. It offers the clear statement that we will be judged at the end of time not for how smart we are, how clever our inventions, or even our sermons, but for whether or not we have directly worked to alleviate individual suffering and structural injustice. We will be judged not first for doing evil, but for not doing good and not serving those most in need.

A Sermon Brief

"When did we *see* you?" I've been thinking about ways we see—*really* see. However, do we come to know God with real understanding if we do not see God reaching into our mundane everyday lives? Unless we long for God, expect God to show up here, however do we come to understand God's presence at all? And then, how do we see biblical stories re-presented today, and see new parables being acted out?

As Rabbi Abraham Heschel has said, when our vision is impaired by negative habits of seeing, or when we're prone to seeing only what we're used to, we can be limited by our expectations and experience, our fears and failings—and we can miss so much. I recognize this each time I visit my son, who's an artist and graphic designer. He sees so much when he simply steps into a day that its humbling to me—but at the same time he also inspires me to want to learn to enlarge my field of vision, too. So I think a challenge for Christians, for all of us here today, is to develop our capacity to expand our vision, to see our reality more clearly, but more important than that, to see God's presence in the midst of our reality here in the city, in others and in ourselves.

The book *Imaging the Word* suggests developing "new eyes for seeing" in a kind of liturgy of three movements. At the first, prayer and the preparation of our souls so that we can receive greater insight is required. Practicing stilling our hearts and attending to the present moment, like intentionally breathing in and out, opens us and extends our capacity to discover and connect to all around us. Prayer or contemplation or simply "opening" is a first movement that frees us to perceive God's presence about us, and prepares us to move beyond superficial seeing. An example of a prayer could be

> I was hungry and you blamed it on the costs of war.
> I was hungry and you circled the moon.
> I was hungry and you told me to wait.
> I was hungry and you said, "so were my ancestors."
> I was hungry and you said, "God helps those who. . . ."
> I was hungry and you told me I shouldn't be.
> I was hungry and you had foreign debt payments to make.
> I was hungry and you said, "The poor are always with us."
> God when did we *see* you hungry?

Meditation, the second movement, can move us beyond simple sight. "What do you think it means?" we ask, entering the spiritual realm of disclosure and revelation, of depth and growing insight. Here beyond the superficial, we may learn to discern God when standing before a burning bush, or passing the color purple by the roadside, or watching God's little ones in our church school. And then, as Blanche DuBois says in *A Streetcar Named Desire*, "Sometimes—there's God—so quickly." Suddenly we see God everywhere—in the homeless man living by our parking lot, in my friends Lonna and Chuck who married yesterday, in a man in Trenton State Prison, in you, in me. And this can be strong and alarming stuff.

"When did we see you God?"

Listen to the story of Angela, by Mev Puleo.

Someone is dying on our campus. A once-beautiful woman is withering away in front of the library, not far from the university's major pedestrian thoroughfare. She has pitched her wasted shell against one of the columns that upholds our reservoir of neatly bound wisdom.

I see her on my way to photocopy chapters of Dom Helder Câmara's work. . . . I see her as I walk toward the beautifully renovated business school to study Max Weber and the benefits of modern bureaucracy, and when I go to visit my challenging companions at the Jesuit formation house, where, over a warm dinner, we discuss faith, politics and poverty.

In psychology class, we talk about neurosis, obsessions and other mental disorders. Outside, she sits clutching her thick, disintegrating Bible with bony, bruised fingers. Huddled in a fetal embrace of her legs, she wedges her restless head between her knees. Her eyes flutter, dart about, then rest on something no one else sees. . . .

Her hair and eyes are more wispy and wild today. And I think she's getting thinner—or so it seemed when I passed her on the way to the student center to change clothes for the evening.

. . . Will she be able to find an urban shelter with room for one more "guest"? . . . Or will she even bother to look beyond this corner she's chosen as her home? . . .

I offered her food once, but she rudely rejected it. She turns away abruptly when I try to talk to her. Not only does she refuse my charity, she repudiates my person. Stung with bitterness, I recoil. . . . For my arrogant anticipation of her gratitude kills the goodness of the deed before it is done. She shuts us out; but didn't we shut her out, long, long ago? . . .

I think someone is dying. Actually, we are all dying; and she—an unseemly prophet—is a constant reminder. . . .

Angela, you're a mirror thrust before us, but can we bear the sight?

The sight of Angela—of God here present in "the least of these"—provokes our third movement, that is our response to what we see, when we see God.

I believe God wills us not to pass by on the other side of the street; that God counts on us to take concrete action from our real resources and strengths. And we can only do that here, in the real world around us. So its here that we learn to see our whole world as spirit filled, and every moment as replete with God's presence, and every person as whole and huy.

"When do we see you? When we feed and clothe and house the least of these who are members of God's family, we do the same to God."

And for our response? We respond in many ways, and especially as we come with new vision to this table. It is set for the feast of Christ the Sovereign, the Christ whose "kingship" was known for breaking the bread for the poor. Here there is a meal for everybody; here the earthiness and tangibility of the elements remind us of bottom-line necessities of life in Los Angeles, in Zaire, in Nazareth and Jerusalem so long ago. As we touch and taste, break and pour and drink, we remember the One who never forgot our common, bodily needs and rejoicing, and whose compassion provokes our work for justice in the community. And there we shall enter God's courts with Thanksgiving.

SUGGESTIONS FOR WORSHIP

Call to Worship

LEADER: Thus say the Lord: I will bring you out from among the people.

PEOPLE: **And gather you into your own land.**

LEADER: And I will strengthen the weak.

PEOPLE: **And the strong I will watch over.**

LEADER: I will feed my people in justice, says the Lord.

ALL: **Praise the Lord!**

Prayer of Confession

God of mercy, we confess that we wish believing the right things was enough. We would like to think that volunteering to hand out the song sheets and polishing the communion cups is pretty much all you call us to. Forgive us for turning a chilly shoulder on the hungry, the imprisoned, the ill, and the homeless. Help us o see Christ in their faces. In his name we pray. Amen.

Assurance of Pardon

Whoever is in Christ is a new creature altogether. The past is finished and gone. In Jesus Christ we are forgiven. Alleluia! Amen!

Benediction (Matt. 25:34 adapted)

Come, my beloved ones, God says. Take your inheritance. In your hands is the kingdom prepared for you from the foundation of the world.

Thanksgiving

Bear Ride Scott

Deuteronomy 8:7-18: In the midst of enjoying God's gracious provisions, the Israelites are cautioned not to forget the Lord.

Psalm 65: Thirteen verses of thanksgiving to God for the goodness of the earth.

II Corinthians 9:6-15: A small stewardship sermon: Mission giving not only supports the needs of the saints but also glorifies God. "God loves a cheerful giver."

Luke 17:11-19: Jesus heals ten lepers but only one returns to thank him.

REFLECTIONS

Just because the act of remembering—*anamnesis*—has played a large role down through the ages in Jewish and Christian worship forms doesn't mean we have gotten very good at it. Present-day Christians anyway, perhaps like the Israelites described in the Old Testament lesson, need to be reminded to remember. In the Hebrew Scriptures the psalmists, the writer of Second Isaiah, and the Deuteronomists are among the best rememberers.

"Remember that you were a slave" (Deut. 5:15), "Remember what the LORD your God did" (Deut 7:18; 24:9), "Remember the wonderful works" (Ps. 105:5), "Remember the former things of old" (Isa. 46:9), "I remember your name in the night, O God," they say.

Tracing the word through the New Testament, we find it used more often in an interpersonal context, "remembering your brother at the altar" (see

Matt. 5:23-24) and "remembering you in my prayers" are more common than "remembering the mighty acts of God." The Gospels, in particular, are not big on the word, although Jesus does say "Remember, I am with you always" (Matt. 28:20). Even there, though, he's mostly using the word the way we tend to use it now—as a way to focus people's attention on what follows. All of this begs the question, Just when did we start taking remembering for granted?

When you think about it theoretically, it is clear that almost any meaningful act of thanksgiving involves remembering. Thanksgiving implies remembering, putting our lives in a larger perspective, and calling to mind our dependence on God. However, when I look back over all the classic middle-American Thanksgivings I've participated in, I'm surprised to realize how adept I've become at a language that focuses on the thanks and minimizes the remembering. I've even been to a couple of Thanksgiving dinners where the thanking is about as thin and dry as the skin on the turkey. Maybe that's the inevitable result of forgetting.

A SERMON BRIEF

In his book on the foibles of our human condition entitled *The Man Who Mistook His Wife for a Hat,* Dr. Oliver Sacks noted an odd complaint from a couple of patients of his. Both cases have to do with slightly deaf women in their eighties who had amazing auditory experiences. One night, Mrs. O'C had a vivid nostalgic dream of a forgotten childhood in Ireland. When she awoke from her dream, she continued to hear the lively Irish music about which she had dreamt. It was the middle of the night. She was puzzled. She checked all her radios, but they were turned off. And yet, the music of her childhood played on.

Mrs. O'M told her story, which began with her grating parsnips in the kitchen. Suddenly she heard a succession of songs: first "Easter Parade" then "Glory, Glory Hallelujah" and finally, "Good Night Sweet Jesus." Like Mrs. O'C, Mrs. O'M was convinced that she had left the radio on, but indeed, she had not. The music followed both women around. Mrs. O'C had once heard that a loose dental filling could transmit radio waves, but then she realized how unlikely that was in that her Irish music was never interrupted by commercials.

Both women found their way to Dr. Sacks, who reported on the difficulty with which he interviewed them, in that they could barely hear him over the din of music playing in their heads. As the diagnosis unfolded, it became clear that the two Mrs. O's suffered from a musical epilepsy called "reminiscence"—a sort of convulsive upsurge of melodies within their heads that could even be trailed by the spikes and valleys of an electroencephalograph, or EEG. It seems that this sort of neurological disorder is the exact opposite of amnesia, of forgetting: It is hypermnesia, or always remembering. They over-remembered. Their brains simply passed along too much information at unwanted times. Hypermnesia.

Perhaps you have already made the connection between Thanksgiving and this story. Thanksgiving is both a patriotic and religious holiday: It is a day set aside by presidential proclamation that we each, in our own way, remember our blessings, count them, give thanks, and pass them on. People of faith would be quick to affirm that this is an appropriate thing to do—a good use of a day in the year—but we would also be quick to point out that truly being grateful, that is, remembering our blessings, counting them, giving thanks, and passing them on, requires more than a day. It requires our entire lives and every moment in them. And would that it could be that we might have the gift of hypermnesia in realizing that it is a gift to focus our very lives on the constant flood of memories, moments, and attitudes of gratitude and praise.

I'm quite certain that the first Thanksgiving was a lovely one—not so much because of the beauty of the fields and forest (for history has it that the fields were rocky and the forest was treacherous). No, that first Thanksgiving's wonder lay in the discovery by people of faith that even in their time of ultimate need (cast ashore in a winter they nearly failed to survive) they were able to make it through, and with the help of the native people of their newfound land, by the next summer they even prospered, and by early fall they figured that they might thrive. In short, they discovered (like people of faith do in every generation) that the God who had led them into the wilderness was also with them through the wilderness. The God in whom the Pilgrims had put their deepest trust remained faithful. And so they gave thanks.

The author of Deuteronomy writes, "Do not say to yourself, 'My power and the might of my own hand have gotten me this wealth' " (8:17). The message of Thanksgiving is that we know in our heart of hearts that it is neither by our power nor the might of our hands, nor by our intelligence nor clever imaginations that we have gotten to where we are (wherever we are), but it is by the grace of God, and so we give thanks.

The grace of God often comes to us, through us; that is, through one another. That is what the Pilgrims learned when they were taught by friendly strangers how to grow corn and where to fish and hunt so they could live through the first winter. And so in discovering that grace, the response of those people of faith was to say thanks, yes, but also *do* thanks—to respond in kind. That should be the challenge of our time as well.

The psalmist knew it too. "Bless the LORD, O my soul. O LORD my God, you are very great. You are clothed with honor and majesty, wrapped in light as with a garment. You stretch out the heavens like a tent, you set the beams of your chambers on the waters, you make the clouds your chariot, you ride on the wings of the wind, you make the winds your messengers, fire and flame your ministers" (104:1-4).

Originally the word "obedience" did not just mean doing what you were told. Originally that word, "ob-audience" meant listening with a heart attuned to life's meaning. So in the strictest sense we are obedient when we—like the psalmist, and like the people of faith of old—listen very carefully to the clues that we get from life, to the clues of the goodness of God and the created wholeness of Creation, and count it as blessings to have our minds, our hearts, and our souls inundated with this input of Thanksgiving that would make us, too, a hypermnesic people of faith—remembering, counting what is good, giving thanks.

"What shall I return to the LORD for all [God's] bounty to me?" asks the psalmist, to which the hymn writer replied, "Were the whole realm of nature mine, that were a present far too small; Love so amazing, so divine, demands my soul, my life, my all." The trick is to remember.

SUGGESTIONS FOR WORSHIP

Call to Worship (Psalm 65 adapted)

LEADER: Praise is due you, O God, you who answers prayer!

PEOPLE: **When our sins overwhelm us, it is you who forgive us.**

LEADER: Happy are those whom you bring near to live in your courts.

PEOPLE: **We shall be satisfied with the goodness of your house.**

LEADER: You are the hope of all the ends of the earth.

PEOPLE: **You crown the year with your bounty.**

ALL: **Let all flesh praise the Lord!**

Prayer of Confession

We are a nation of forgetters, O God. As a people, as a church, as a community we find it difficult to remember our histories. Worse still, we fail to see your hand in our stories. Accounts of your mighty acts are handed down to us by our grandmothers, and we let them grow cold. Tales of your gracious ways are handed down to us by our grandfathers and we let them sit idle. Our children do not know how much thanks they owe you. Forgive us. Fill our minds and hearts with your Spirit, and our mouths with thanks. In Jesus' name we pray. Amen.

Assurance of Pardon

God's mercy is from everlasting to everlasting.
Friends, believe the Good News.
In Jesus Christ, we are forgiven.
Alleluia! Amen.

Charge and Benediction

Rejoice always, pray constantly, and give thanks in all circumstances. And may the love of God, the grace of our Lord Jesus Christ and the power of the Holy Spirit fill our hearts and minds. Now and forevermore. Amen.

Contributors

Joanna M. Adams, Pastor of Trinity Presbyterian Church in Atlanta, Georgia. A sought-after speaker, Joanna has preached at the General Assembly of the Presbyterian Church and was a member of the committee that drafted the denomination's newest creed, "A Brief Statement of Faith."

Jean Alexander, Pastor of Bethesda United Church of Christ in Bethesda, Maryland. Having just passed the twenty-fifth anniversary of her ordination, Jean writes, "For someone who didn't think she would make it past year two, this seems like a cause for celebration. Even though there are days I would rather not be a minister, the call to preach keeps me going. Given that I currently have two teenagers and a toddler grandson in my house, that is saying something."

Minerva Carcaño, Director of the Mexican American Program at Perkins School of Theology, Southern Methodist University in Dallas, Texas. An ordained elder in The United Methodist Church, she is a team officer of the General Conference Connectional Process Team and serves on the Board of The United Methodist Publishing House. Minerva and her husband, Tom Spaniolo, have a daughter, Sofia.

Susan Halcomb Craig, Pastor of United University Church on the campus of the University of Southern California in Los Angeles. A freely feminist woman of faith, Susan reimagines a fully inclusive church.

Joanna Dewey, Associate Professor of New Testament Studies at the Episcopal Divinity School in Cambridge, Massachusetts. She also performs the story of Mark's Gospel in "Women on the Way: A Feminist Retelling of Mark."

{ Contributors }

Cynthia Hale, Pastor and founder of Ray of Hope Christian Church in Decatur, Georgia. Beginning ten years ago, with only four persons meeting for Bible study, the church has welcomed more than two thousand members to date, making it the fastest growing Disciple church in Georgia. Dr. Hale is a member of the African American Biographies Hall of Fame and a 1993 recipient of the Martin Luther King Board of Preachers' award.

Esther Hargis, Pastor of First Baptist Church in Berkeley, California—a historic church of the American Baptist Churches, USA. She has been an ordained minister for twenty-three years, but she's been a serious mystery fan her whole life (well, practically).

Edwina Hunter, Professor of Preaching at Union Theological Seminary in New York. Co-editor (with David Albert Farmer) of *And Blessed Is She* (Harper & Row, 1990), Edwina was one of the first women in the country to hold a full-time tenured position as a seminary professor of homiletics. Many of this generation of women preachers refer to her affectionately as "the mother of us all." After her retirement in 1997, she plans to make her home in sunny Santa Rosa, California.

Barbara Lundblad, Pastor of Our Saviour's Atonement Lutheran Church in New York City. Barbara says that though she is, at heart, a farmer with roots in the Iowa soil where she grew up, she also has a deep and abiding love for New York City where she has been a pastor for sixteen years. She spends as much of the summer as she can in Deer Isle, Michigan, living in a converted white-frame country church and searching out new islands in her kayak.

Beth Merrill, Associate Pastor of the First Presbyterian Church in Springfield, Illinois. She is grateful to her many teachers who encouraged her to think and grow, to her congregation who inspires her to greet life with honesty and hope, and to her cats, Sophie and Bud, who remind her to stretch out and take a nap once in a while.

Anne Miner-Pearson, Rector of All Souls' Episcopal Church in San Diego, California. A love of learning and preaching has characterized her thirteen years in the ordained ministry and led her to the completion of a Doctor of Ministry degree in 1995. Anne's life includes mothering, grandmothering, power walking, and a ministry of hospitality with her husband—an Episcopal priest and a gourmet cook.

Amy Miracle, Associate Pastor of Central Presbyterian Church in Denver, Colorado. She enjoys biking, hiking, skiing, playing the piano, and cheering on the Colorado Rockies.

{ *Contributors* }

Bear Ride Scott, Director of Student Affairs on the southern campus of San Francisco Theological Seminary located in Claremont, California. Having pastored several Presbyterian congregations over the last seventeen years, Bear has turned her attention to preparing the next generation of ministers.

Mary Donovan Turner, The Carl Patton Associate Professor of Preaching at Pacific School of Religion in Berkeley, California. She is an ordained minister in the Christian Church (Disciples of Christ) who is mother of two, spouse of one, and friend of many.

Diane Turner-Sharazz, Instructor in Homiletics at the Methodist Theological School in Delaware, Ohio. Diane has pastored churches in the East Ohio and West Ohio conferences of The United Methodist Church. She is presently a candidate in homiletics and New Testament at Vanderbilt University. In addition to teaching, she directs and plays piano for the seminary's gospel choir.

Scripture Index

Subject Index

{ *Subject Index* }